LISS, HAMPSHIRE © Vicki Couchman

THE UK AT HOME
PROJECT WAS
MADE POSSIBLE
THROUGH THE
GENEROSITY OF

British Library Cataloguing-in-Publication Data:
A CIP record for this book is available from the
British Library

ISBN: 978-1-84483-652-9
10 9 8 7 6 5 4 3 2 1
Printed in China

First published in the United Kingdom
and Ireland in 2008 by

Duncan Baird Publishers Ltd
Sixth Floor
Castle House
75-76 Wells Street
London W1T 3QH

ISLE OF SKYE, INVERNESS-SHIRE *Earth, water and
Skye*. The rugged beauty of Scotland's coastal islands has
been home to the Clan MacLeod since the twelfth century.
Family descendants still inhabit Dunvegan Castle, the
oldest continuously inhabited castle in Europe. Other
island residents include not only those whose families
have lived on Skye for generations, but also incomers from
across Britain looking for an alternative to the bustle of
twenty-first-century life. 📷 Richard Baker

UK AT HOME

A CELEBRATION OF WHERE WE LIVE AND LOVE

CREATED BY RICK SMOLAN & JENNIFER ERWITT
AGAINST ALL ODDS PRODUCTIONS

dbp

DUNCAN BAIRD PUBLISHERS
LONDON

BROADFORD, ISLE OF SKYE *Visionary.* Apart from a period studying in Glasgow long ago, Barbara Christie, 58, has lived all her life in Swordale House, which overlooks Beinn Na Caillich (The Hill of the Old Woman). A drastic reduction in Skye's population began in the late eighteenth century as landlords evicted crofters (smallholders) and introduced sheep farming in what became known as the Highland Clearances. Now the population is edging up towards 12,000 with incomers attracted by the scenery, and tourism helping job prospects for the islanders. 　📷 Richard Baker

ORFORD, SUFFOLK *Effervescent.* Samphire Mitchell-Cotts, 19 months, catches bubbles with her sister, Tamarisk, 8. Their family recently moved to this idyllic spot and, unlike Tamarisk, little Samphire has adapted quickly to her new home, and will likely remember no other. 📷 Caroline Irby

INTRODUCTION

FOR ME THE WORD 'HOME' IS ONE THAT CONJURES UP so many emotions. My own earliest memories are filled with a warmth and security that come from a good family environment.

The word can also conjure up not so pleasant memories — friction, arguments, the sadnesses of growing up and for parents, just trying to keep a family together. But these memories seem to fade as time goes by, leaving a positive feeling in their place.

Home is a place to return to, set off from, tell your tales in, air your grievances in, share your joy in. It means different things to each one of us but for me the warmth and strength of my home is always foremost 'no matter where I roam'.

In this book, there are many examples of the meaning the word 'home' has to various people, and my particular connection to this book is via the photography work of my daughter Mary, who is one of the contributors. When I think of home, I naturally have memories of her from birth until now and it warms my heart to think of the many precious moments we've spent together and now she is following in the footsteps of her Mum and taking beautiful pictures. I think this also validates the importance of home life.

Although I know many people who were unlucky enough when they were growing up not to have a good home life, many of them have now made good homes for themselves and have escaped the trap which they so nearly succumbed to. In Liverpool when I was growing up, my formative years were filled with family, uncles and aunts, friends circulating through our house and making it into a very warm place to spend time in. Later, when I travelled abroad, it was always very rewarding to come home and switch off, knowing that my family would completely understand and welcome me back.

I hope that your memories of home are good ones or that the meaning of the word in the future will become special and as reassuring as it can be. Home is where the heart is. There's no place like home. Home sweet home. It's the best place to be.

Paul McCartney

Paul McCartney has been inducted into the Rock and Roll Hall of Fame both as a member of the Beatles and as a solo artist.

BRIGHTON, EAST SUSSEX *Home turf.* Tania and Greg Schnuppe relax amid the chimney pots on their tiny rooftop terrace, while their sons, Ben (on bike), 4, and Max, 5, play on a neighbour's terrace. In densely populated Brighton, many houses lack conventional gardens, so people carve out hundreds of little patches — complete with artificial grass, potted plants and sea views — on their rooftops. ◉ Roger Bamber

POWYS, WALES *Maintaining their dignity.* Gareth Davies, 54, and his wife, Alison, 53, live in one of the most isolated farms in Wales. Their modernised sixteenth-century farmhouse in Powys has no mains electricity. They have been campaigning against wind farms for 12 years and although they have no wind turbines on their own land, they are surrounded by them. The couple have also just learned that a major road is to be built close to their home. ◎ Steve Peake

STEPNEY, LONDON *All the world's a stage.* Todd Longstaff-Gowan (left), an architect and landscape garden designer, has a serious interest in the history of collecting. He and Tim Knox (right), curator of the Sir John Soane's Museum, have sought to create a home art collection that evokes the feel of the great private museums of the past, arranging their treasures in a deliberately theatrical manner. Here, amid a decade's worth of collecting, the pair entertain neighbours Katharine Goodison (right) and Phoebe Lewis with pheasant pie and fine wine. © Barry Lewis

SEVEN SISTERS, LONDON *Girls' night in.* A group of friends who have shared life's highs and lows together for years celebrate at the home of photographer Vicki Couchman who took this picture. She says: 'We dance together, eat dinner together, holiday together and laugh and cry together. We are blessed with our meeting of like minds. Our husbands are friends, our children are friends, and we belong to a very special group of wonderful, kind-hearted soulmates.' ◎ Vicki Couchman

THE MYSTERY OF HOME

LIFT UP THE LIVING ROOM CARPET, the threadbare one, to replace it or to run a telephone cable underneath it. Avert your eyes from the places where it has grown so shamefully thin and look at what lies underneath. Old linoleum, perhaps, as a reminder of the fact that one's lucky to have a carpet at all; old linoleum produced by those long-gone mills in Fife that produced lino for the whole of Britain, and underneath that... newspapers. The papers were placed there to give some backing to the lino, and they are yellowed but otherwise preserved. Lift them up. Unfold them. *King Abdicates. Allies Cross Straits of Messina. Soviet Freighters Steam towards Cuba*. Layers of history.

The people who put the newspapers there had no idea that they were planting time capsules. Nowadays time capsules have a rather contrived air to them: posed photographs, messages of greeting and so on. The informal time capsules you find in the house are simpler, more reflective of ordinary life, things not specially singled out, but eloquent in their testimony to a particular moment. The old newspapers under the floor place the house at an identifiable day. On the day below the newspaper masthead, that actual Wednesday 5th June or whatever the date on it, on that day the people who lived in this house, the people who laid the carpet, were thinking about the events in the paper, were living through them. There is a poignancy in that, particularly since we know the outcome. We know about the pampered, socialite existence that would be lived by the Duke of Windsor, we know that the Allies would make it to the top of Italy, we know that the Soviet freighters would turn back at the last minute and that jumpy commanders' fingers would stay away from the button that could have vaporised it all, including this house. But there is another poignancy: the lives of the people who lived in the house then are probably over, or nearly over. Houses survive generations of occupants: we are ultimately all temporary tenants — never permanent owners.

The house's mystery reveals itself in so many other ways. Many very ordinary houses in Britain were built a century ago, if not earlier, and so the doing of domestic archaeology is not something limited to those who can afford to live in expensive older buildings. These Victorian and Edwardian houses often conceal the evidence of earlier tastes in decoration — contoured anaglypta wallpaper, dark varnishes, here and there the piece of stained glass that must have added to the general gloom. But it's not just taste that is revealed when wallpaper is stripped back: the hand of the workman is also shown. Pencil markings on the wall — measurements, lines — make up the signature of those who built the house or decorated it. These markings have a sense of intimacy about them. We may not know the name of the workman, but we sense his presence. I feel this particularly strongly when I look at the details of old woodwork. Somebody cut that piece of wood a long time ago, made those saw-marks, slotted home those joints. Who was he? An apprentice working under supervision? A skilled joiner? And who was it who stood in this place, in this room, one hundred and twenty years ago and nailed the floorboards down or fitted this window frame — and sometimes also fitted that very bit of glass, with its irregularities and uneven thickness? And it has all survived; survived the knocks and jolts of day-to-day life in the house; survived world wars, the fall of empires. He who made it would not have imagined that any of those things could happen. If you live in a Victorian house in Britain, then the people who made it probably believed that their world would last for ever. Perhaps that's why we accept impermanent architecture today, why we often don't build things to last: we no longer believe that anything *will* last.

But the pleasure of doing this domestic archaeology is not limited to the fabric of the house itself. There is a particular fascination to finding out who lived in the house before you, your predecessors in title. The deeds, of course, will tell you something about that. These documents, couched in impenetrable legalese, and written — in the case of earlier deeds — in painstaking copperplate, reveal who sold the house to whom. Or left it: houses pass from hand to hand through the generations, by power of wills drawn up to prefer the claim of this person against that, this dutiful daughter against that profligate son. Resounding family arguments are concealed in tiny phrases; virtue rewarded, debts of honour recognised. And much social detail is casually included: widows may be described as *relicts*, left behind on this shore by the departing husband. Lesser relatives may be given small interests: the right to remain in the house until their death, or their marriage or whatever condition defeats them.

In the study of my Victorian house in Edinburgh there is a mantelpiece. This Swedish marble mantelpiece has a history: it is not the original, but was put there by the man who owned the house in the early 1950s , a well-known Edinburgh fireplace manufacturer. He had one son, David, who spent his childhood here in this house. David had a model cathedral, complete with models of priests and bishops. Somebody later told me that a number of the toy bishops were buried in the garden. Why? We shall never know; the son is dead, as are the parents. That's a secret that the house will keep. A mystery.

Above the Swedish marble mantelpiece there hangs a large formal portrait of a woman dressed in black, looking rather like Whistler's mother. The portrait was there when we bought the house and has remained in its place. I was told that the woman in the picture was the widow of a nineteenth-century Edinburgh lawyer, whose daughter bought the house from the fireplace manufacturer. Recently I took the portrait down and found an envelope tucked into the back of the frame. A considerate hand had written on the envelope: *about this picture*. Inside, a note gave the name of the artist, a nineteenth-century Scottish portraitist by the name of Macbeth. It also gave the name of the vaguely disapproving woman in the picture.

Of course every attic has its secrets. Our neighbours, when they acquired their house, found a box in the attic which was filled with draft letters in the hand of the elderly woman who had lived there before them. There was something special about these letters — they were anonymous. She was an anonymous letter-writer who had spent hours composing draft letters for every occasion, including one to neighbours on the other side of the road who had taken to hanging washing out on the *front* lawn. That, the draft anonymous letter said, was not how things were done in this street.

Our attic revealed a plan of the house under the regime of those who immediately preceded the fireplace manufacturer. In those days the house belonged to a charitable trust, which ran it as The Edinburgh Home for Babies and School of Mothercraft. That was its official name, but it was widely known as a home for fallen women, those being the days in which women fell. The fallen women came here to have their babies and be instructed in the art of looking after them or helped to hand them over to adopting parents. Every room is identified in this plan: my study was the lecture room in which the fallen women were presumably lectured on how to avoid future falls. Our bedroom was matron's room, and I can imagine that matron, can hear her.

Of course not every house has quite that colourful a history. But even a more prosaic history will have its mysteries. The people before you, the ones from whom you acquired the house, will always leave some trace of their existence, even if they have been scrupulously careful about clearing up before they left. How soulless are hotel rooms by comparison with houses: nothing is left of the previous occupants — or nothing we can see; their DNA, of course, lies all about, including the pillow on which the next guest lays his head. But houses are different — there will be little signs of the last occupants, raising all sorts of questions. What was the extra, unidentified key found hanging on the back of the door? Whose photograph is under the gas boiler? What were they celebrating when they opened the empty champagne bottle found in the shed? And were they celebrating *in* the shed? Post arrives, too, for the long departed. Catalogues reveal their tastes; the occasional telephone call comes through. The detritus of other people's lives attached in some curious way to this physical place; every bit of it capable of raising some questions, evoking some reflection on how we occupy our homes on loan, so to speak.

We are temporary occupants. No matter how we seek to impress ourselves on place, place smiles knowingly: I am the one who will still be here when you are not. We are possessed by the homes we live in: we think we possess them, but they possess us. ▢

Alexander McCall Smith is an emeritus professor of medical law and author of The No.1 Ladies' Detective Agency *series.*

CAMDEN, LONDON *Water bed.* Songwriter Alice McLaughlin, 28, and film producer Jules Cocke, 29, have been a couple for a year, though they had been best friends for a decade. Alice bought her 53ft narrowboat several months ago. 'It's very chilled-out and open-plan, very simple, with a bath right in the middle and the bed at one end. Being here is like being on holiday,' says Alice. 'There's no central heating, just a coal-burning stove, so you have to work hard to keep it cosy in the winter.' 📷 Leonie Purchas

SHEPHERD'S BUSH, LONDON *Separate chores.* On Saturday morning in the Clark household, Flora, 8, practises for her grade one level violin, but dreams of playing the saxophone. Meanwhile, her sister, Eliza, 10, who is more interested in music than housework (she is on grade three on the flute and is learning the cello), unenthusiastically sorts out the washing as part of her weekend chores. Edmund Clark

SHERBORNE, DORSET *Wall papered.* Saskia Tempest-Radford, 13, is one of 328 boarders at Sherborne School for Girls. Saskia says a lot of the girls come to her room for tea and a chat after lessons; it's become a popular hang-out. 'When I go in my room, it feels like home,' she says. 'I have pictures of family and friends all around me.' Established in 1899, Sherborne is an independent day and boarding school. 📷 John Downing

[Seventy-four percent of UK households own a car. Forty-six percent have two.
Five percent have three or more. More than 18 million workers travel to work by car
each day, spending an average of 58 minutes a day behind the wheel.]

HM NAVAL BASE CLYDE, FASLANE, DUNBARTONSHIRE *Pacified.* The Faslane Peace Camp
was set up outside the gates of HMNB Clyde in 1982 to oppose the presence of nuclear weapons at
the base. Britain's longest-running peace camp, it currently has 10 full-time residents. Fifty-two-year-
old Matt Bury, who has been at the camp for a year, decorated his caravan himself. He also recently
installed a wood burner. 📷 Richard Baker

WHITWELL, ISLE OF WIGHT *Monster.* Paul Scott Rolfe's pick-up truck swamps the bungalows on either side and fills the driveway of his mother's house. His Nissan Navara is one of a limited edition of only 300 made to celebrate Nissan's entry to the 2004 Dakar Rally. Paul, 38, bought it in part-exchange for his old pick-up. There are four similar Navaras on the Isle of Wight, but only two are red — and Paul and the driver of the other one regularly exchange nods when they pass. 📷 Vicki Couchman

Over the last 35 years, the number of people in the UK who prefer to live alone more than doubled, from 3 million to 7 million.

DONCASTER, SOUTH YORKSHIRE *Splish splash.* 'It's nice to live in a place that you've done up yourself,' says Neil Rands, 45. Originally a builder, Neil is now studying art and has already sold several of his paintings. 'This is my bedroom-cum-bathroom-cum-chilling room and it's my favourite room in the house,' he says. 'I like to get out some candles and a glass of wine and relax.' 📷 Guilhem Alandry

BLACKDOWN HILLS, DEVON *Feet first.* Will Brown, 33, braves the cold all year round to keep clean. A tree surgeon, he built his remote house seven years ago from trees he felled himself. His friend Tom 'Briggsy' Briggs, 30, can be seen inside the house, which Will shares with his black mongrel, Scoobie. Will pays the farmer who owns the land a nominal rent and often barters his labour for essential goods. 📷 Andy Hall

HACKNEY, LONDON *Camera shy.* It is estimated that the traveller population in the UK is currently about 300,000. Predominantly Roma gypsies of Indian descent, their numbers also include Irish and Scottish. Travellers are recognised as a distinct ethnic group under British law. They have a strong sense of community, to the extent that they have their own dialects and unique customs. Whether they live in houses or caravans, the plain exteriors of travellers' homes often belie sumptuous interiors. ◎ Gideon Mendel

SEVEN SISTERS, LONDON *Table topping.* Kiki Honey Mei Lett, nearly 3, stands on a bench in her family's back garden. She's laughing at her friend, a blackbird, who visits the garden every day. Behind Kiki is an amateur attempt at repairing the fence. 📷 Vicki Couchman

EBCHESTER, COUNTY DURHAM *Lift yer feet.* Nina Barr, 50, and her husband, Mick Marston, 58, have lived in their Victorian terraced house in a former mining village for more than 20 years. They bought and knocked through the house next door when their daughter Rowanna, now 16, was born and they needed more room. 'It's a very strong community,' says Nina. 'A lot of people have lived here for a long time. We both love the garden and Mick can spend all weekend out there.' 📷 Zak Waters

HOVE, EAST SUSSEX *It's all in hand.* An inspirational and popular English teacher in a busy comprehensive school, Sab Sahota-Lyons, 35, also has three small children. Although Sab lost her sight as a child to Still's disease, in 2001 she was named Teacher of the Year at the Pride of Britain Awards. 📷 Pål Hansen

In touch. Sab has developed a range of skills for coping with the sighted world, from washing up to teaching, since losing her sight at the age of 8. At school, Sab recognises every pupil by voice and takes the morning register with a computer. Like any other teacher, she writes on the whiteboard with a pen. And an assistant reads student essays aloud to her. 📷 Pål Hansen

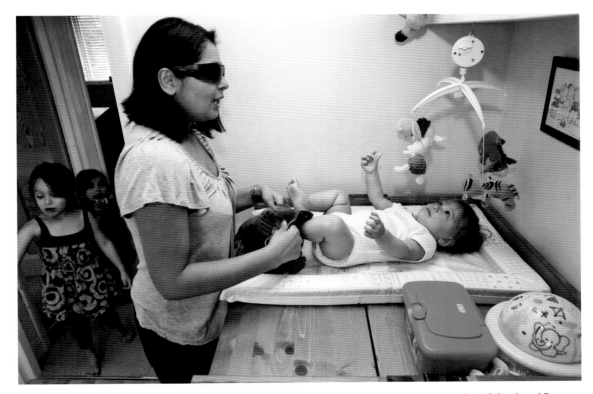

A practised hand. Besides being a full-time teacher, Sab is also a black belt in karate — and, with husband Dean, the mother of three: Ella, 4, Jaia, 2, and nine-month-old Liah. 'The kids are exactly the same for me as anyone else,' says Sab. 'During nappy-changing Liah will wriggle around, which is why we've got a mobile above the mat to keep her occupied.' 📷 Pål Hansen

ABERGAVENNY, MONMOUTHSHIRE **Magic kingdom.** Kailash Pinnock, 7, sets up toy soldiers on the sill inside the thick walls of his family's fourteenth-century keep-house and barn, nestled into a cliff in the Black Mountains. 'The landscape is magical,' says his mother, Petra, 37, who shares the home with her husband Gavin, 38, Kailash, and daughter Tara, 10. 'It's a perfect place for free spirits to roam.' 📷 John Downing

DUNGENESS, KENT **Warmobil.** On a cold and foggy day at his family's weekend home in a converted coastguard tower overlooking the beach, Felix Marlow, 8, prepares his Playmobil characters for battle. 📷 Peter Marlow

[Life expectancy in the UK today is approximately 30 years longer than it was 100 years ago. A male child born in 2008 will live approximately 76 years. Girls live even longer, with an expected life span of 81.]

HOLLOWAY, LONDON *Scale model.* Since she was 4, Najeeya Dew-Najah, now 9, has divided her time between the homes of her divorced parents. In order to ensure that children maintain strong relationships with both parents, more divorced or separated couples are co-parenting in this way, with children dividing their time equally between two homes — meaning two bedrooms, two sets of clothes, two sets of everything. Here, at her father's home, Najeeya likes taking care of her lizard, Harry. 📷 Thomas Brandi

NEW CROSS GATE, LONDON *Glow of health.* In her home, Amber Sibley, 39, a make-up artist and colour therapist, adjusts a light table (the first of its kind in the UK) that she developed with an American colleague. Light therapists believe that by altering the lights that surround us, it is possible to enhance health and well-being. They often combine the use of colour with other complementary therapies, such as aromatherapy, massage, reflexology and yoga.   Mike Goldwater

CHARLTON, LONDON *Aqua marine.* 'My duck's name is Drake,' says Jessica Hall, 12. 'My Granny and Grandpa got it for me when I was three and it makes my bath times so much more fun. Whenever I have a bath, I switch the light off and watch it change colours.' Says her father Andy, 'She loves that duck — despite being told by everyone that she's too old for it.' 📷 Andy Hall

STRATFORD-UPON-AVON, WARWICKSHIRE *Box seat.* As they move from one theatre to another, actors spend a lot of time living in digs, sometimes for months at a time. Tom Davey, 28, is currently performing in *Twelfth Night* with the Royal Shakespeare Company at the Courtyard Theatre in Stratford-upon-Avon. Here he rehearses in the afternoon for the evening performance, in which he will play an officer, a house guest and a sailor. ◉ David Levene

HERSTMONCEUX, EAST SUSSEX *Pics for pickers.* Polish workers sleep four to a room at Greenway Fruit Farm during the fruit-picking season. 'Farmers need to wake up,' says Graham Love, who took over the farm from his father in 1971. 'The climate is increasingly difficult to predict, oil is expensive and things are going to get worse. To survive we have to adapt.' During harvest season, 15 workers sleep in Graham's house, his bedroom included, while he sleeps in his office. 📷 Peter Dench

ORFORD, SUFFOLK *Bouquet.* Nineteen-month-old Samphire Mitchell-Cotts plays beneath the washing line in the garden of the house into which her family recently moved. Samphire and her five siblings — Celandine, 11, Tamarisk, 8, Campion, 7, twins Rowan and Valerian, 4 — are all (apart from Rowan) named after the wild flowers that grew on the beach and in the garden at their former Suffolk home by the sea. 📷 Caroline Irby

OXBOROUGH, NORFOLK *The family moat.* Henry Bedingfeld feeds the swans from a window at Oxburgh Hall, a stately moated manor house built by his ancestor in the fifteenth century. Henry lives in several rooms reserved as family quarters. The National Trust has managed the rest of the property since the 1950s. Henry is the York Herald at the College of Arms, the government office that regulates heraldry. 📷 Stuart Freedman

OXBOROUGH, NORFOLK *Hearts and flowers.* 'On 14 February 1477, my ancestor John Paston received a letter from Bridget Coke in which she called him "My Valentine",' says Henry Bedingfeld. 'That is apparently the first use of this term in English, and it gave birth to a great British tradition. They married and I am therefore directly descended from these two, the first two sweethearts to call each other Valentines.' ◎ Stuart Freedman

The arms and the man. Henry's position as York Herald — officer of arms — at the College of Arms dates back to the fourteenth century. The salaries for heralds were amended by William IV in 1830 to reflect the living costs of the day but have never been adjusted for inflation — so today Henry receives the princely sum of £17.80 per annum. 📷 Stuart Freedman

LEEDS, WEST YORKSHIRE *Tucked in.* Keith Ward, 49, has suffered from health problems for most of his life. After living for a long while with his elderly mother, he recently moved to the Faith Lodge Hostel to benefit from its care. Residents are provided with their own rooms and three cooked meals a day. In exchange, they are expected to work 15 hours per week around the house. They can stay indefinitely so long as they get along with other residents and don't drink. 📷 John Angerson

[Clergy rank themselves amongst the happiest people, by profession, in the UK.]

DEEPING ST JAMES, LINCOLNSHIRE *Warm blessings.* The Reverend Mark Warrick, Vicar of Deeping St James, 53, has led his parish for ten years. He is required to live in the parsonage while he holds his post. 'It is a very comfortable home and is a sanctuary to some extent,' he says, 'but parish priests do not really expect a real sanctuary. Everyone knows my address and telephone number and my "office" is in the house. But then, I've never sought a refuge from the world.' ◉ Charlie Gray

ORFORD, SUFFOLK *Lonely leap.* The Mitchell-Cotts family used to live in a cottage by the sea, but with six children they were bursting at the seams and so have recently moved a mile inland to a larger house. Tamarisk, 8, a wild spirit, pictured here leaping from one room to another, misses her old home. A note written by her, pinned to the kitchen noticeboard, announces to her parents: 'I HATE LIVING IN THIS HOUSE. I AM NOT FREE.' Caroline Irby

LIVERPOOL, MERSEYSIDE *Oasis.* Madryn Street is where Ringo Starr grew up. Now, residents are being forced to move out as the council demolishes the houses. 'I wanted to stay because it has been my home for 32 years and is a lovely little house,' says Sandra Graham, 62. 'It was a smashing neighbourhood and very friendly. Now I am waiting to move to a new house around the corner. The nice thing is I will be joining five of my old neighbours.' 📷 Andrew Buurman

HAPPISBURGH, NORFOLK *On the edge.* Twenty-five houses in this village have been lost to coastal erosion since 1990. Diana Wrightson's home, 40 metres from the cliff a decade ago, is now just five away and she has to evacuate with every storm. 'It could go tonight, it could happen in a year,' she says. 'There is no insurance coverage, the house is worthless. We've lost everything but there are no regrets.' Erosion will cause an estimated 13,000 hectares of English shoreline to disappear over the next 20 years. 📷 Stuart Freedman

KNARESBOROUGH, NORTH YORKSHIRE *Stony stare.* Graciela Williams, who is in her sixties, lives in a home built into a rock in 1770 by a gentleman named Thomas Hill. Thomas spent nearly 17 years constructing his unusual habitat which was then inhabited by generations of the Hill family who lived there until Graciela purchased it in 1996. 'Surprisingly, the house is very warm,' she says. 'It's very compact, but also atmospheric and peaceful and has inspired me to write my poetry. I believe the knight by the front door is twelfth century and from a sacred site. It is certainly much older than the house.' 📷 Guilhem Alandry

KNARESBOROUGH, NORTH YORKSHIRE *Rock of ages.* A conservation architect, Graciela, originally from Mexico, spent her career restoring historic churches in Mexico and now restores buildings on her late husband's estate. 'I have always loved stone buildings and have researched the behaviour of stone and written a book about it,' she says. 'As the house is Grade 1 listed, it's difficult to make improvements because planning permission for even the smallest repair is hard to obtain. For example, I can't access the bottom of my garden and am still using a ladder as a consequence!' 📷 Guilhem Alandry

ISLE OF SKYE *Leppard's lair.* Tom Leppard, 72, has lived in an underground hut on a remote corner of Skye for 22 years. He had himself tattooed with leopard spots all over his body following 28 years of service in the Royal Navy and the Army. Tom's hut is protected from the elements by a strong tarpaulin on the roof and the entrance is a narrow stone slot, with a fabric curtain used as a door. ◉ Richard Baker

ISLE OF SKYE *Singular.* Very few people know the exact whereabouts of Tom and his home, and those who do protect his privacy. Tom keeps his hut meticulously neat and bathes each day in one of two nearby streams. 'I decided I wanted to be the biggest of something, the only one of something,' he says. 'It had to be a tattoo.' Tom is recognised in the *Guinness Book of World Records* as the most tattooed man on Earth. ◉ Richard Baker

10:03 AM

10:05 AM

10:07 AM

10:13 AM

10:14 AM

10:16 AM

HOUNSLOW, MIDDLESEX *Final approach.* In 1894, the president of the Royal Society, Lord Kelvin, stated that heavier-than-air flying machines were impossible. Today, Michael Ward spends the majority of his days wishing Lord Kelvin had been correct. Forty years ago, when Michael moved to his house near Heathrow, the air traffic over his home was manageable. But these days it's a living nightmare for Michael and his neighbours, who are forced to deal with planes that roar overhead every few minutes from early dawn to late into the evening. According to the BBC, an estimated 258,000 residents currently experience Heathrow noise levels greater than 57 decibels, the level at which the government begins restricting noise. An additional two million residents, some living as far away as Maidenhead and Richmond, experience noise levels above 50 decibels. In an interview with the BBC, John Stewart, who heads the 25,000-member

10:09 AM

10:11 AM

10:12 AM

10:17 AM

10:18:AM

10:20 AM

Heathrow Association for the Control of Aircraft Noise (HACAN) ClearSkies, explains why local residents are up in arms: 'The one place you feel you can escape from the bustle of the world is your own home. Once you shut your door, that's it: you have shut out the world. But this noise invades every part of your home, almost every part of your being — and you just feel there is no escape.' ClearSkies, formed in 1999, first caught the attention of the national media when members (pretending to be house buyers) discovered that more than half of estate agents selling homes in the area 'forgot' to mention that certain properties were under the flight path. And the situation is only going to get worse: plans are now under way to construct a third runway and sixth terminal at Heathrow, which some advocates claim may cause 4,000 homes to be destroyed and force as many as 10,000 people to find new places to live. 📷 Chris Steele-Perkins

FOXTON, LEICESTERSHIRE *Long alone.* Fernley Tancock, 52, a retired mechanical engineer, has lived on his houseboat on the Grand Union Canal since 2002 when he moved back from South Africa. While Fernley spends most of the time alone on the narrowboat, once a month he travels to Exeter to visit his wife Margaret, a nurse, and to see his 30-year-old daughter Lisa. 📷 Thomas Brandi

FOXTON, LEICESTERSHIRE *Marine life.* 'It's as snug as a bug in here in the winter,' says Fernley. 'These boats have everything you need on them these days and are very comfortable.' Fernley lives with his Jack Russell terrier cross, Louis. 'I've seen quite a lot of the country,' he says. 'Birmingham, Manchester, Peterborough, Oxford. . . There really is no better way to see England than in a boat.' 📷 Thomas Brandi

ROTHERHITHE, LONDON *Albatross.* Furkan Choudhury, a college lecturer, motors his dinghy towards his converted barge in the South Dock marina. First-time sailors often don't realise how important it is to secure a mooring before buying their boats and can find themselves perpetually cruising the waterways network. In London it can take three years or more to find a mooring.　📷 Mike Goldwater

SOUTH DOCK MARINA, LONDON *Room with a view.* Simone Wood, 40, has lived on her ex-Royal Navy boat for two years. She and her brother, who is a marine carpenter, took those years off work to restore the boat. 'It's better than living in a house,' Simone says. 'It's the freedom; and the people around are very friendly.' The boat has two showers, two loos and sleeps seven, although Simone spends quite a lot of the time there alone. Her boyfriend, Tom, has his own boat. 📷 Mike Goldwater

SHEPHERD'S BUSH, LONDON **_Her mistress's voice._** Eliza Clark, 10, practises the flute, while her sister Flora, 8, lies on the sofa, watching Saturday morning television. Minty, their border terrier puppy, looking embarrassed in her head funnel, guards both. 'We moved into the house 11 years ago, before we had kids,' says their dad, Ed, 'and we're still trying to do the place up.' 📷 Edmund Clark

SHEPHERD'S BUSH, LONDON **_Rise and shine._** Flora (left), Eliza, and Lucy Clark, 42, at breakfast time. 'The sense of 'home' is so much more than bricks and mortar,' says Lucy, 'and this house will always be special as the place where our second daughter arrived in an unplanned home birth.' Lucy's arrival in the kitchen this morning was also so unexpected that her husband, Ed, photographed her in her dressing gown. 📷 Edmund Clark

PECKHAM, LONDON *Off the register.* Schools exclude children if they have seriously broken the rules or are a threat to other students. Sadly, many of those who are excluded come from the most vulnerable communities and often simply disappear from the education system. More than 9,000 children were excluded in England last year. 📷 Simon Wheatley

LLANRWST, CONWY, NORTH WALES *Eye to eye.* When her parents divorced four years ago, Megan Murray, 9, found herself with two bedrooms. This one, in her mother's house, is quite tiny, with room for little more than a bed. Her bedroom at her father's house is much larger. Happily for Megan, the television programmes are the same at both places. 📷 Roger Hutchings

HM NAVAL BASE CLYDE, FASLANE, DUNBARTONSHIRE *Side show.* David Reynolds, aka 'Eco', has been an activist and campaigner for many years. He has made his home at the Faslane peace protest camp for the past three years. David's house, known as the Earth Shack, is made almost entirely from scrap found on local rubbish tips. His mother was a 'carnie', a carnival worker, and David suspects that's why he enjoys his alternative lifestyle. ◉ Richard Baker

PONTEFRACT, WEST YORKSHIRE *Location location location.* The 115-metre-high cooling towers at Ferrybridge C Power Station, the largest of their kind in Europe, loom over nearby homes. The towers first helped supply energy to the National Grid in 1965 but a year later, during gales gusting up to 85 mph, three of them collapsed. Even though they had been built to withstand high wind speeds, their shape funnelled the wind into the towers themselves, creating a devastating vortex. The towers were rebuilt and all eight were strengthened to withstand bad weather. Barry Lewis

SOUTHWARK, LONDON *Block party.*
Unemployment among the residents
of flats on the Brandon estate is high,
but so are spirits: a recent Children and
Youth Festival drew 500 people without
a single disturbance. Its costs were paid
for by TV shows filmed in the area —
including *The Bill, Doctor Who,* and *Spooks*
— which frequently use the estate to
portray urban realism. The block, built in
1957, has 68 flats and the residents are
primarily low-income, young, multi-ethnic,
single-parent families. ◉ Brian Griffin

SOUTHPORT, LANCASHIRE *Slice of the past.* Preserving a small piece of Britain's engineering heritage, Brian Madden, 56, runs the British Lawnmower Museum. He has more than 500 in his collection, the oldest from 1850. 'Lawn mowing is a very British thing,' he says. 'In other countries they just do grass cutting. With mowing, the lawn is rolled and striped flat.' Brian's preferred choice for his own lawn is a 1930s hand-operated mechanical mower.   📷 Ivor Prickett

WEALD OF KENT *Sunset shadows.* Nestled deep within the Weald of Kent, 30 miles south of London, a fifteenth-century house set in 60 acres radiates peace and tranquillity. The house looks out over mature trees and manicured gardens which have flourished here for centuries. 📷 Rick Smolan

WOKING, SURREY *After the fast.* Mufti Liaquat Ali Amod, 52, and his wife Zainub, 45, prepare a meal to break the Ramadan fast. They fast for a whole month, every day from daybreak until sunset. Ramadan is the ninth month of the Islamic lunar calendar and the holiest of the four holy months. The spiritual aspects of the fast include refraining from gossiping, lying, and slandering. Purity of thought and action is paramount.   📷 Charlie Gray

[After Christianity, the second most common faith in the UK today
is Islam — espoused by nearly 3 percent of the population. Mohammed is currently
one of the 20 most popular names for boys born in England and Wales.]

Door keeper. Mufti and Zainub have five children, four still living at home. They live in two flats on the mosque site. As well as raising the family, Zainub teaches Arabic and Islamic history. Daughter Ayesha, 16, is at school. 'We all look up to our dad, he's very lovely,' Ayesha says. 'It's also nice to have our own flat upstairs. It's our own little place, a hideout.' ◎ Charlie Gray

Purification. Mufti, imam and head of education at the Shah Jahan Mosque, prepares for prayer. 'We wash our hands first and brush our teeth,' he says, 'then clean our nose and whole face, then the right arm and left arm up to the elbows. Then we pass our wet hands over our head, neck and ears and wash our feet, first the right then the left. Then we wipe our feet and go to the mosque to pray, which we do five times a day.' ◎ Charlie Gray

HAMPSTEAD GARDEN SUBURB, LONDON *The final stretch.* A refugee from Nazi Germany, who moved to England in 1980, Rose Mendel is now 84. Though active and very fit, she has recently developed some health problems, including deterioration to her spine (which Pilates somewhat helps to alleviate). It is a difficult time for her as she is about to move out of the home she has lived in for the past 28 years. 📷 Gideon Mendel

In preparation. 'I'm not exactly looking forward to moving,' says Rose Mendel, 84. 'My house is old and very comfortable, but I have no choice. I'll miss my garden. I just love walking in it, planning, and messing around.' Her new home will be a warden-controlled flat in Highgate. Her grandson Michael, 26, an academic, visits about three times a year from Newcastle. 📷 Gideon Mendel

Looking back. The thought of leaving home evokes many memories in Rose who, at the age of 15, was separated from her family for many months at the beginning of World War II. Rose, who lived in Germany, was travelling on a freighter to Cape Town from England (where she had been an exchange student) to join her family, when war was declared. Her ship was rerouted to Spain where Rose spent three months before she managed to catch another boat south and join her family. Rose returned to England as an adult, this time to stay, 28 years ago. 📷 Gideon Mendel

DUNGENESS, KENT *Shingle style.* Formerly a coastguard tower built in the 1950s, this weekend retreat for photographer Peter Marlow, Fiona Naylor and their children stands on the shingle beach. Dungeness is of international conservation importance — one of the largest expanses of shingle in the world and home to a rich variety of plants and wildlife. But it is also home to two nuclear power stations. 📷 Peter Marlow

Coast watch. Fiona and two of her three boys, Theo, 3, and Felix, 8, read in the top-floor bedroom, once the observation room of the tower. The house, converted in 1996, sits right next to one of the power stations. 'We're not particularly bothered by the power station next door,' says Peter. 'It's no worse than living downwind of the same site in central London.' Peter Marlow

DUNGENESS, KENT *Pylon.* Felix Marlow launches his model aircraft off the roof of the converted coastguard tower. In the background is the Old Lighthouse — the fourth of five in the town's history — which opened in 1904. It was rendered obsolete by the construction of the nearby power stations. 🖸 Peter Marlow

Airborne. Fiona, Felix and Theo fly a kite on the shingle. 'There is something of a playground feeling to Dungeness,' says Fiona. 'We all seem to merge into the landscape and briefly forget about all the things we get up to in the city. That's why we love to spend our weekends here.' 📷 Peter Marlow

LEICESTER, LEICESTERSHIRE *Midlands masala.* Pushba Mortaria, 64, prepares vegetable curry for her family. Pushba came to England from Uganda with her husband, Vanu, in 1972, and currently lives with her son, his wife and her grandson. More than a third of the people in Leicester are new or second-generation immigrants. By 2012, the city will be the first in the UK in which ethnic minority groups are in a majority. 📷 Vicki Couchman

Song and dance. Priyen Mortaria, 8, Pushba's grandson, watches a Bollywood movie. India produces about 850 films a year, or an average of more than two per day. That's almost double the number made by Hollywood — and the popularity of these romantic glimpses of the old country continues to rise among British Asians. 📷 Vicki Couchman

Distant faces, distant places. At her bedroom shrine, Pushba prays every day to relatives who have passed away. Their faces intermingle with family photographs and other personal mementos. 📷 Vicki Couchman

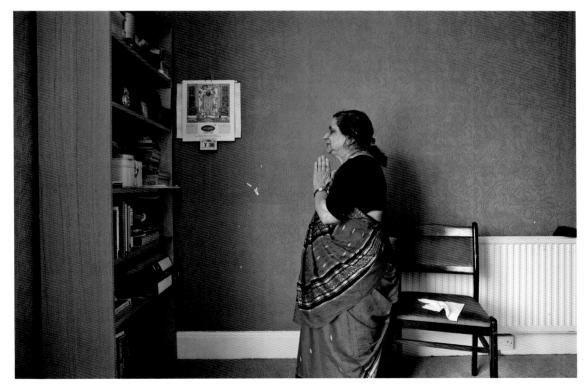

The dear departed. At a shrine between two wardrobes in her bedroom, Pushba practises Puja prayers and gives thanks to the Hindu gods daily as well as remembering relatives who have passed away. Pushba was born in Uganda, but left in 1972, when the dictator Idi Amin gave all 80,000 Asians there three months to get out of the country. Some 30,000 of those expelled fled to Britain, many having had to leave their wealth and possessions behind. 📷 Vicki Couchman

[Women in the UK now make 80 percent of home improvement
decisions and 60 percent of DIY purchases.]

POLLOK, GLASGOW *Endless vigil.* Rose Gentle, 43, sits in the garden with her mother, Pauline Graham, 67. Rose's son Gordon was killed by a roadside bomb in Basra in June 2004. A painfully long-delayed inquest into her son's death concluded that a failure in the Army's supply chain meant he did not have the piece of equipment that would have saved his life — it was sitting in a storeroom less than a mile away. To honour her grandson's memory Pauline collects donations and items for under-equipped soldiers in Iraq. Since his death, Rose has become a ferocious anti-war campaigner. 📷 David Modell

KENTISH TOWN, LONDON *Consolation.* Tracey Flack, 38, and Vanessa Lopes, 28, met five years ago in a nightclub. Today they live in a flat above Tracey's veterinary practice. 'I love my work,' Tracey says, 'although it can be stressful when dealing with sad cases — like putting down animals that you have looked after for a long time. But it can also be very rewarding: I operated on a dog today and now it's making a good recovery.' When it all gets too much, she heads upstairs to wind down with Vanessa. 📷 Dario Mitidieri

EAST DEAN, WEST SUSSEX *Family circle.* Rosie O'Brien, 8, makes tea over a wood-fired stove on a visit to her father, Mike, 49, in his yurt home. Mike built the yurt and pitches it as he moves from place to place. 'I'm a bit of a nomad,' he admits. Originally from Central Asia, yurts have been adapted for different cultures and are often lived in by people seeking a more sustainable way of living.   ◎ Roger Bamber

[First-time buyers saw the average price of a home rise by 204 percent between 1995 and 2005. The average cost of a house in November 2007 was £230,474.]

EAST DEAN, WEST SUSSEX *Lattice.* Mike and Rosie O'Brien gaze out of the clear plastic window. Yurts are increasingly popular in the UK and are used in all sorts of ways, from garden offices to summer houses, from wedding marquees to party tents and wendy houses. For Mike, yurts are both his home and his job: he earns his living building them, as well as tipis, pavilions and other fabric-based structures. 📷 Roger Bamber

LANDIELO, CAERNARVONSHIRE *Without corners.* Dani Lee-Smith, 32, escaped a hectic life in London, with her partner, Simon, 46, three years ago. They have three children under seven. Dani says a yurt is much more comfortable than a house because there are no hard edges. The Tipi Valley community where they live, sharing land and resources with about 100 people, was established in 1970. 📷 Steve Peake

> " The average Briton has 8–14 close friends, more than 80 contacts on his mobile phone and at least one Harry Potter book in his home. "
>
> – Tim Wardle, *In Search of Mr Average*

STOW-ON-THE-WOLD, GLOUCESTERSHIRE *Drake and hen.* Adam Tatlow, 38, is head gamekeeper on an estate in Gloucestershire. Here, his daughter Faye, 10, who would like to be a vet, helps him pluck birds. 'She helps me out, and both my children come along with me when I go stalking deer,' says Adam. 'We keep some of the pheasants for ourselves but the rest go off to Belgium. They eat a lot of funny stuff out there, including horse, and they're mad on hares.'   John Downing

Fowling peace. Adam has been a gamekeeper since leaving school at 16. The house comes with the job. Despite the standard image, Tatlow says he rarely has trouble with poachers; they sneak on to the estate perhaps once a year. 'It's usually done at night with a lamp so you tend to see them,' Tatlow says. 'We tackle them and then get the police involved.' 📷 John Downing

CHADWELL HEATH, ESSEX *Family affair.* Jack and Phyliss Ringer-Hewitt have been together for 70 years. Both in their nineties, they met when their parents married, so making them step-brother and sister. That didn't stop them falling in love, and on New Year's Day, 1938, both aged 22, they married. They were given their house as a wedding present and have lived there ever since, keeping it almost unchanged. 📷 Duncan Raban

MALVERN, HEREFORDSHIRE *Fish and friends.* Tony Fletcher, 54, visiting from London, tucks into a plate of fish and chips with his friend Ian Wells and Ian's wife Lisa. Tony and Ian met at their first job after university in 1977 and have remained friends. 'Do we usually have fish and chips?' asks Tony. 'Never! In fact we only had them on this occasion because we had been out mountain biking and got back late.' 📷 Zak Waters

DAGENHAM, ESSEX *Ethiopian Roast.* Ras Brenton, 55, and his son Emanuel, 10, roast coffee beans brought home from a recent trip to Ethiopia. Ras runs a record studio and music centre in Hackney. It's a place for creating CDs for musicians, listening to reggae and playing pool. A Rastafarian, Ras has been to Ethiopia several times and wants to start his own music studio there. 📷 Pål Hansen

FORTWILLIAM, BELFAST *A full helping.* Cathy and Hugh Russell, both 45, have four children. Here they are sitting down for supper with their eldest son, Hugh, 20, and Cathy's mum, Elizabeth, 82, who is visiting. Meanwhile, Max the family dog lurks below. 'We're very boring!' says Hugh. 'We're all pretty easy going and all get along well.' 📷 Justin Kernoghan

[Thirty years ago, after having a baby, mothers in the UK took an average of 6.7 years before returning to work. Today the majority of mothers go back to work in 2.3 years.]

MAYFIELD, EDINBURGH *Baby bonds.* Anna Scott, 35, with her two-day-old son, Murray. Anna met her partner, Robin, also 35, at a speed-dating event. 'What drew me to Robin was that we just had a spark together and also his lovely nature,' she says. 'We both feel we were destined to meet each other. And now Murray is part of our lives and it's as if he has always been there. He's fab! He was the best present ever. He was unplanned, a surprise, but a wonderful one.' Cecilia Magill

LEITH, EDINBURGH *Lines and curves.* Catherine Lazcano-Thornton, 29, is six months pregnant with her first child. Self-employed, she runs a cleaning agency and a textile design company. She hopes to keep both businesses going after the baby is born. 'I'm a little bit anxious about the birth,' she says, 'but it's getting more real now.' Cecilia Magill

WALWORTH, LONDON *Born again.* Marie Johnson, 53, and her husband David, 63, Pentecostal Christians, brought their family to London from Nigeria seven years ago. Now Marie would like to return home. The estate where they live is often used to exemplify urban decline; reportedly a crime takes place there every four hours. 'When you're an immigrant, your self-worth as an individual hits a low,' says Marie. 'You have to start from scratch.' 📷 Simon Wheatley

DUMFRIES, DUMFRIESSHIRE *Devotion.* Monk Sherab Zangmo and nun Ani Rinchen Khandro prostrate themselves to the Buddha in the main temple of the Samye Ling Tibetan Monastery in Eskdalemuir. Established in 1967, Samye Ling was the first — and is still the largest — centre of Tibetan Buddhism in Europe. The monastery serves not only as a permanent home for monks and nuns, but also as a temporary residence for members of the public who are on retreats. 📷 Murdo MacLeod

SIMON WINCHESTER

THE TRINKETS OF EXPATRIATE LIFE

TODAY WAS THE FIRST TRULY cool day of autumn — by the first light of morning I could still see the ice tossed out from last night's party sparkling, unmelted, on the lawn — and so I was more than glad the Aga had kept the kitchen cosily warm overnight. I fumbled with the computer in the early gloom and switched on Radio 4 — *The World This Weekend* was just beginning.

I opened up a fresh box of Scott's porridge oats and added the requisite amount of water and salt, and while that was simmering, started the rest of our usual Sunday breakfast: two boiled eggs from our own hens, a quiver-full of soldiers, Kerrygold butter, Marmite, whole-wheat toast and Cooper's Oxford marmalade, two cups of Twinings English Breakfast tea. And then, as the second cup began to cool, the paper — the *Times*, of course. No, not that *Times*, but our local: the *New York Times*, the quarter ton of newsprint that is dumped out of a delivery truck before dawn each Sunday, and which will take us most of the coming week to read.

For our Sunday breakfast, as much a simulacrum of Britishness as we can make it — Aga to Twinings and all points in between — is conducted today as it invariably is each Sunday in our ancient farmhouse in a tiny village in the Berkshire Hills of western Massachusetts. The party we held yesterday was both to celebrate my birthday and to press the first cider apples of the season, the leaves around us a riot of oranges and yellows and glorious gold, and with the local farmers promising us that from the look of our maple trees there'll be a good sugar flow this winter and we'll have gallons of maple syrup to collect when the snow is six foot deep upon the ground. There are few places more American than the village where my wife and I choose to live out our remaining days; there are few places more British than the kitchen where we choose to begin each one.

I have spent most of my adult life wandering around the world. Aside from a spell in the early Eighties when I was based in Oxford —

but even then travelled endlessly, the bag at the end of the bed ever-packed in case my foreign editor telephoned to tell me to head off to some temporary trouble-spot: Cairo, Bangladesh, the Falkland Islands — I have not lived in England since 1970.

For well-nigh 40 years I have lived away. I have had homes in various parts of the cities and hinterlands of Belfast, Washington, New Delhi, New York and Hong Kong, each one of them for many years at a time, and in each of which I have done my best to create a feeling of settlement and temporary permanence. And now I have settled, and for good I think, in America. For a while I kept a cottage on a tiny island in the Western Isles of Scotland, a talisman of Home: but even that has gone now, and when I come back to Britain, as I do half a dozen times a year, I stay in hotels. Home I have to accept is now my farm in Berkshire County, together with a flat in Manhattan: and each seems, unwittingly I like to think, to have accumulated itself into an outpost of the country I have long left behind.

Although Sunday breakfast springs to mind as a memorial to longing, it is perhaps the more trivial of the touchstones — it is merely a ritual, like listening to the Christmas Broadcast or the Boat Race, which offers up no more than the briefest of sensual connections. It is in the various rooms of the house that are the more solid props — spiritual, intellectual, nostalgia-producing — that keep me most firmly rooted and recognised as a Briton living abroad.

Our farm's small Keeping Room, for example — the phrase comes from colonial times, when the family would keep itself in the one warmed centre of the house — has on its ancient shelves, I note, the following small and sorry amassment of tokens that have followed me around the world: a well-scuffed cricket ball from a game I once watched in the Oxford University Parks; a platoon of toy soldiers (Grenadiers, I think); a clutch of crystals of Derbyshire Blue John; a silver Georgian teapot with an ebony-wood handle; two Dinky toys — one a white Land-Rover Defender (a scale model of the real one that

I keep parked outside the barn, and which I rarely use as it drinks one now very expensive gallon of petrol every 12 miles), the other an MGB; a collection of old British penny pieces, each so heavy one realises just why holes-in-pockets were an affliction of the British Fifties; an old spool of Cash's name-tapes with my school number, 46, machined in blue on white; a pile of pub beer-mats and two ashtrays, one from an inn at the southern end of Loch Rannoch, the other marked LNER, and presumably from some station waiting-room — Grantham, I suspect, or perhaps the deliciously remembered little halt named Drem — on the East Coast Main Line.

Given my childhood obsession, long cast off, there are all too many reminders of railways scattered round the house: a pair of GWR station clocks, one in the kitchen, another in my study; old timetables, solid bosses of brass that performed branch-line functions now long forgotten, sepia photographs of tank engines standing in their sidings at Maiden Newton and Castle Cary, a ticket showing the fare from Paddington to Dorchester West as ten-shillings-and-eightpence, and in the bathroom reading-baskets copies of *Steam Trains Monthly*, along with *Sea Breezes*, *The Smallholder* and *The Scots Magazine*.

There is an irony here, of course. The Britain that I once seemed to miss so very much out here is only a remembered Britain, a country of my cigarette-card collecting, *Eagle*-reading youth, an idealised and very different country of the past. When I go home I try gamely to cling on to it: I stay in a small, privately owned hotel in Marylebone, all brass stair-rods and teak panelling, with hunting prints in the bedrooms and Fougasse cartoons in the loo, with scones and honey each afternoon at three, and never once the employment of a tea-bag, even if asked.

But then I step outside, and as I do so modern Britain — the globalised, multicultural, Tesco, *Big Brother*, Top Shop, Health-and-Safety conscious Britain — is on vivid, urgent display, and I realise in an instant that what I have established in my mind and in our house as my Little-Britain-in-America is really much more *Vicar of Dibley* and *Last of the Summer Wine* and *Brief Encounter* Britain, and not today's *Little Britain* Britain at all.

I first travelled overseas out of curiosity, as do most. But then I stayed away because, quite simply, I thought — and I still think — that life outside Britain can be very much more interesting and satisfying and rewarding than an existence pinioned in the comfort of home. Especially the home that today's Britain offers me. I love my life in America. I wake each morning cheerful and eager for the day ahead. I am on the way to becoming a citizen, and soon I shall come back to Britain less and less frequently, as the need within subsides.

But as I slowly and steadily detach myself, shall I need to hold on to all my talismans?

This is what my wife — who is American, and of Japanese origins — keeps asking me. Do I really need that dusty old cricket ball? Or those lumps of brass that remind me of *The Titfield Thunderbolt*? Or the ashtrays that make visitors suspect we smoke — which, quite religiously, we don't. And isn't the bathroom copy of *Steam Trains Monthly* actually a senior's version of *Playboy* in another guise? Britporn, she calls it jokingly, saying I linger over it far too lovingly.

She's winning, as she inevitably must. This time a year ago I owned two Land Rovers: now one has gone, and has been replaced by a Toyota, and a hybrid at that. I no longer have either sugar or cream on my porridge, and once in a while I have *miso* soup at breakfast. (My wife, however, loves Bird's custard powder and makes a meanly alcoholic trifle.) Because my wife worked for National Public Radio I find we listen to that more frequently than we do to Radio 4. I have stopped my subscription to the *Spectator*. I listened to a baseball game the other day, and found I had forgotten who England were playing in the latest Test.

Slowly, surely, Britain is slipping from my grasp. I have put down roots in the oldest corner of the New World, and am attaching myself entirely to its systems and its customs. In a year or so I will be able to vote in its elections — and at the moment of first doing so I will, I know, cast off one of the final emotional attachments to home. The cricket ball will probably go soon after; the Defender will head at last for the scrapheap; I'll give the Dinkies to a neighbour's child.

Soon, I suspect, only the old cream-coloured Aga will remain, warm and immovable in our cosy farm kitchen. That, and framed in the library, the certificate signed by the Queen, of the OBE that she kindly gave me at the Palace last year. Those I'll keep always: two sweet reminders of Home, in a place very much Away. Or rather: two reminders of Away, in a place that is now very much Home. 🏠

Simon Winchester is the author of The Surgeon of Crowthorne *and* Outposts: Journeys to the Surviving Relics of the British Empire.

FEOCK, CORNWALL *Bon voyage.* Anne and Nick Barwell host a lunch party for friends about to depart on a tour to the Galapagos Islands. Nick, 70, a retired consultant surgeon, is the Commodore of the Royal Cornwall Yacht Club, which organises local races and, every four years, a 2,400-mile race to the Azores and back. The Barwells host about six such luncheons per year — often moving out into the garden, where they can look out over Carrick Roads, a popular sailing area. 📷 Simon Roberts

" Love, friendship, family, respect, a place in the community, the belief that your life has purpose—those are the essentials of human fulfillment, and they cannot be purchased with cash. "

– Gregg Easterbrook

FEOCK, CORNWALL *Generations.* Anne Barwell sits with her 22-month-old granddaughter, Isabella, who is fascinated by the toy dog (which sings when its paw is squeezed). 'Our home is a very important part of all our family's lives,' says Anne. 'Our children all live outside of Cornwall and really value the time they can spend here, as they all enjoy sailing. It's a very happy home with a lovely atmosphere.' Simon Roberts

The ultimate host. Nick Barwell opens another bottle of champagne. The garden, which he and Anne carefully tend, is about three-quarters of an acre and contains a number of tender plants that wouldn't survive in Britain outside Cornwall's mild climate. 'We like having parties,' says Anne, 'and when our children come home they like to gather their friends here as well.' 📷 Simon Roberts

STOKE NEWINGTON, LONDON *Street scene.* Neighbours gather for the second annual Belfast Road junk sale and street party. Usually the street is empty except for parked cars, but this is the one time each year when the road is closed, music played, food served, stalls set up — and the residents have an excuse to hang out together. 'Opportunities to get together with your neighbours are becoming rare, especially in the city,' says one local. The atmosphere is alive, warm and mischievous — much like the people of Belfast Road. 📷 Leonie Purchas

THORNTON HEATH, LONDON *Cinderella.* Andrea Narveaz-Buitron, from Ecuador, prepares for her 15th birthday party. 'In South America when a girl turns 15 she enters womanhood,' says Andrea. 'You look forward to this day from when you are a little girl. You wear pink silk slippers to show that you are still a child. Then during the ceremony your father changes them to high heels to show you are maturing.' 📷 Thomas Brandi

Team work. 'A lot of my friends are Latin and understand the tradition,' says Andrea. 'They are basically a second family to me and we were all so excited as we got ready. My 16-year-old Colombian friend Dave was my dance partner. My seven girlfriends wore baby-blue dresses and their dates all wore suits with blue silk tops.' 📷 Thomas Brandi

Childhood's end. 'Your parents also give you lots of presents including a Bible and a ring to show their never-ending love,' says Andrea. 'The ring my parents gave me was made of gold with two hands holding each other — when you open it a heart comes out. I was also given a doll to help me remember this special day.' 📷 Thomas Brandi

> " The average Briton drinks three cups of tea a day, believes in God, is more than £3,000 in debt, is captured on CCTV cameras 300 times a day and drives a Ford Fiesta. "
>
> – Tim Wardle, *In Search of Mr Average*

FINCHLEY, LONDON *Up and away.* Harold Gittleman, 45, takes time out with his two daughters, Emily, 15, and Gabriella, 12, before they head off to a family event. Harold is managing director of a company that runs shops and spas on cruise ships. During the week he works in Bristol and comes home on Thursday nights. For the next three days the family tries to do everything together — the cinema, ice skating and big Sunday lunches. 'We stay in touch the rest of the week by texting and Facebook,' Harold says. 📷 Charlie Gray

KINGSWINFORD, STAFFORDSHIRE *Indomitable.* Pat Reeves, 61, works out beneath some of her many trophies. Pat holds regional, British, European and World titles and has been British powerlifting champion for 15 years. 'There are many reasons why I do it,' she says. 'It shifts the focus away from my health problems and empowers my spirit. I strongly believe the difference between the impossible and the possible lies in a person's determination.' Kalpesh Lathigra

CLAPTON, LONDON *Global gathering.* The Budi family, Muslim immigrants from Gujarat, India, gather for an evening meal to break the Ramadan fast. 'Coming together with our family during Ramadan is a blessing,' says matriarch Rehana Budi. 'Through fasting we realise what it is like for poor people. We avoid worldly things and become more connected spiritually through prayer.' Throughout the holy month of Ramadan the family watch only Islamic television, which broadcasts live the scenes from Mecca in Saudi Arabia. 📷 Gideon Mendel

HENDON, LONDON *Atonement.* Lubavitch Hasidic rabbi Gershon Overlander and his wife Sarah-Leah prepare for the ritual of Kaporos, performed on the eve of Yom Kippur. This ritual involves circling a live white chicken around a person's head three times, while reciting a Hebrew prayer, as a way to symbolise atonement for one's sins. 📷 David Levene

MARBLE ARCH, LONDON *Cantor.* Lionel Rosenfeld and his wife Natalie, both 60, light candles at the beginning of the Sabbath. Born into a family of rabbis and cantors, Lionel is known as the Singing Rabbi and regularly sings for Jonathan Sachs, Britain's Chief Rabbi. He is in constant demand to conduct Jewish weddings around the world. 📷 Barry Lewis

STAMFORD HILL, LONDON *Keeping kosher.* Rachel, Yosef and Yacon Rosenberg, 2, 4 and 6, sit in their Satmar Hasidic Jewish family's *sukkah* — a temporary room built for Sukkot, also known as the Feast of Tabernacles. During the week-long festival, this Yiddish-speaking family will eat their meals in the *sukkah*, which must be built with a roof of leaves and branches, and kept partially open to the sky. 📷 David Levene

POUGHILL, CORNWALL *To love and cherish.* Sarah James, 28, prepares for her wedding. With her are friends Jane Alty, 30, Laura Haworth, 16, and, seen in the mirror, Alison Curry, 36. 'I was terrified when I was getting ready,' says Sarah. 'Not about getting married, but of walking down the aisle and saying my vows — because when I'm nervous I can't speak. But when I walked through the door I caught sight of Nick, and from then on I just smiled and laughed all day.' 📷 Kalpesh Lathigra

STRATTON, CORNWALL *Roasted and toasted.* Groom Nick Younger, a 32-year-old script editor, carries a pig roast through the village with his best man and brother, Dan, 29. 'Nick decided he wanted to look like Doctor Who or a farmer and got a second-hand suit from Camden Market,' says bride Sarah, 28, behind them. 'I was a bit dubious but it worked brilliantly. I danced down the main road in Stratton with my umbrella and people were coming out of the shops to look at us with our pig.' 📷 Kalpesh Lathigra

HACKNEY WICK, LONDON *They clicked.* Photojournalist Andrea Testoni, 34, and Eduardo Martino, 38, dance at their wedding. Shortly after Andrea came to the UK from Brazil in 2004, a friend gave her the email address of Eduardo, another Brazilian photojournalist who had formerly been a mechanical engineer. They met, fell in love and, after the wedding at Hackney Town Hall, celebrated with a party at a friend's home-cum-studio. A second, religious, ceremony will take place in Brazil. 　Guilhem Alandry

BLEDLOW, OXFORDSHIRE *Home team.* Zoe Gullett, 24, is training to be a member of the British equestrian team for the Olympics in 2012. 'I live and work at the same place which makes my life much easier,' Zoe says. 'But it can also be difficult to relax because something always needs to be done. Luckily I do what I love — and it is a privilege to look out of my bedroom window and see my horses grazing or playing.' 📷 Mike Abrahams

APSE HEATH, ISLE OF WIGHT *Gnome Alone.* The first garden gnomes were made in Germany in the mid-1800s where terracotta figurines reflected local myths about gnomes' willingness to tend gardens at night. Garden gnomes were first introduced to the United Kingdom in 1847 and became popular garden accessories. So popular in fact that they became the target of pranks as liberators stole and returned them 'to the wild'. Here a garden gnome takes advantage of a picture-perfect day to relax on the front lawn of a home on the Isle of Wight. 📷 Vicki Couchman

ALAIN DE BOTTON

THE IDEA OF HOME

FOR A WORD THAT CARRIES INTIMATE associations of sanctuary and relief, 'home' seems riddled with a remarkable number of incoherencies and paradoxes.

To begin with, home is almost always a place that we don't appreciate when we are there. Its omnipresence makes it invisible. Think about how differently we approach 'abroad' as opposed to 'at home'. We approach new places with humility. We carry with us no rigid ideas about what is interesting. We irritate locals because we stand in traffic islands and narrow streets and admire what they take to be meaningless details. We risk getting run over because we are intrigued by the roof of a government building or an inscription on a wall. We find a supermarket or hairdresser unusually fascinating. We dwell at length on the layout of a menu or the clothes of the presenters on the evening news. We are alive to the layers of history beneath the present and take notes and photographs.

Home on the other hand finds us more settled in our expectations. We feel assured that we have discovered everything interesting about our house and our neighbourhood, primarily by virtue of having lived there a long time. It seems inconceivable that there could be anything new to find in a place which we have been living in for a decade or more. We become habituated and therefore blind.

But if we leave home and end up in an alien and frightening environment, how soon we remember home — and with what fondness! The only time we really 'see' our homes and recognise their value is when we aren't in them — just as we might only truly feel the love we have declared for our spouses when they are away from us, or when they are dying. Deprivation quickly drives us into a process of appreciation — suggesting that one way to better appreciate something is to regularly rehearse its loss.

To all this we can add the thought that our need for a home arises out of a vulnerability and a lack of solid identity. Our sensitivity to our surroundings may be traced back to a troubling feature of human psychology: to the way we harbour within us many different selves, not all of which feel equally like 'us', so much so that in certain moods, we can complain of having come adrift from what we judge to be our true selves.

Unfortunately, the self we miss at such moments, the elusively authentic, creative and spontaneous side of our character, is not ours to summon at will. Our access to it is, to a humbling extent, determined by the places we happen to be in, by the colour of the bricks, the height of the ceilings and the layout of the streets. In a hotel room strangled by three motorways, or in a wasteland of run-down tower blocks, our optimism and sense of purpose are liable to drain away, like water from a punctured container. We may start to forget that we ever had ambitions or reasons to feel spirited and hopeful.

We depend on our surroundings obliquely to embody the moods and ideas we respect and then to remind us of them. We look to our buildings to hold us, like a kind of psychological mould, to a helpful vision of ourselves. We arrange around us material forms which communicate to us what we need — but are at constant risk of forgetting we need — within. We turn to wallpaper, benches, paintings and streets to staunch the disappearance of our true selves.

In turn, those places whose outlook matches and legitimises our own, we tend to honour with the term 'home'. Our homes do not have to offer us permanent occupancy or store our clothes to merit the name. To speak of home in relation to a building is simply to recognise its harmony with our own prized internal song. Home can be an airport or a library, a garden or a hotel.

Our love of home is in turn an acknowledgement of the degree to which our identity is not self-determined. We need a home in the psychological sense as much as we need one in the physical: to compensate for a vulnerability. We need a refuge to shore up our states of mind, because so much of the world is opposed to our allegiances. We need our rooms to align us to desirable versions of ourselves and to keep alive the important, evanescent sides of us.

It is the world's great religions that have perhaps given most thought to the role played by the environment in determining identity and so — while seldom constructing places where we might fall asleep — have shown the greatest sympathy for our need for a home.

The very principle of religious architecture has its origins in the notion that where we are critically determines what we are able to believe in. To defenders of religious architecture, however convinced we are at an intellectual level of our commitments to a creed, we will only remain reliably devoted to it when it is continually affirmed by our buildings. In danger of being corrupted by our passions and led astray by the commerce and chatter of our societies, we require places where the values outside of us encourage and enforce the aspirations within us. We may be nearer or further away from God on account of what is represented on the walls or the ceilings. We need panels of gold and lapis, windows of coloured glass, and gardens of immaculately raked gravel in order to stay true to the sincerest parts of ourselves.

But without honouring any gods, a piece of domestic architecture, no less than a mosque or a chapel, can assist us in the commemoration of our genuine selves. Imagine being able to return at the close of each day to a beautiful home. Our working routines may be frantic and compromised, dense with meetings, insincere handshakes, small talk and bureaucracy. We may say things we don't believe in to win over our colleagues and feel ourselves becoming envious and excited in relation to goals we don't essentially care for.

But, finally, on our own, looking out of the hall window onto the garden and the gathering darkness, we can slowly resume contact with a more authentic self, who was there waiting in the wings for us to end our performance. Our submerged playful sides will derive encouragement from the painted flowers on either side of the door. The value of gentleness will be confirmed by the delicate folds of the curtains. Our interest in a modest, tender-hearted kind of happiness

will be fostered by the unpretentious raw wooden floor boards. The materials around us will speak to us of the highest hopes we have for ourselves. In this setting, we can come close to a state of mind marked by integrity and vitality. We can feel inwardly liberated. We can, in a profound sense, return home.

We value certain buildings for their ability to rebalance our misshapen natures and encourage emotions which our predominant commitments force us to sacrifice. Feelings of competitiveness, envy and aggression hardly need elaboration, but feelings of humility amid an immense and sublime universe, of a desire for calm at the onset of evening or of an aspiration for gravity and kindness — these form no correspondingly reliable part of our inner landscape, a rueful absence which may explain our wish to bind such emotions to the fabric of our homes.

A beautiful home can arrest transient and timid inclinations, amplify and solidify them, and thereby grant us more permanent access to a range of emotional textures which we might otherwise have experienced only accidentally and occasionally.

There need be nothing preternaturally sweet or homespun about the moods embodied in domestic spaces. These spaces can speak to us of the sombre as readily as they can of the gentle. There is no necessary connection between the concepts of home and of prettiness. One can feel at home in a place which is very unhomely. One could feel at home in a diner or a motorway café with others similarly lost in thought, similarly distanced from society: a common isolation with the beneficial effect of lessening the oppressive sense within any one person that they are alone in being alone. The very lack of domesticity, the bright lights and anonymous furniture can be a relief from what may be the false comforts of a so-called home.

What we call a home is merely any place that succeeds in making more consistently available to us the important truths which the wider world ignores, or which our distracted and irresolute selves have trouble holding on to. 🏠

Alain de Botton is the author of The Consolations of Philosophy *and* The Architecture of Happiness, *among other works.*

BROCKLEY, LONDON *Cheeky.* Oliver Foster-Vets, Ethan Mizen, Ben Swan, Sam Winter, Matthew Swan and Domi Pellew at Ben's ninth birthday party. 'The only way to get boys to pose for pictures is for them to be either super cool or super silly,' says Ben's mother, Caro. 📷 Caro Swan

[UK primary school classes, with an average of 26 pupils, are bigger than almost every other industrialized nation.]

CAMDEN, LONDON *Sling shot.* Rosario Marti, 34, takes a self-portrait with daughter Catalina, 10 months. A journalist, Rosario is currently a full-time mum. Her husband Ricardo says, 'Rosario was thrilled when the baby sling arrived in the post. She went out twice as much just to show it off.' 📷 Rosario Marti

CROUCH END, LONDON *My time.* Breakfast in the bath is a favourite ritual for Caitlin Smail, 47. 'It's a bit of a luxury,' she admits. 'Being in the bath is "me" time because I don't get much of that. I never, ever, have a shower!' 📷 Caitlin Smail

> " Home is a name, a word, it is a strong one; stronger than magician ever spoke, or spirit ever answered to, in the strongest conjuration. "
>
> – Charles Dickens

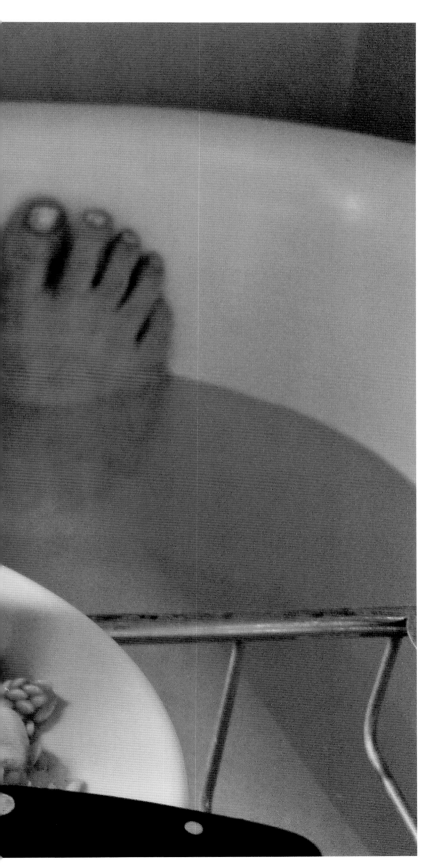

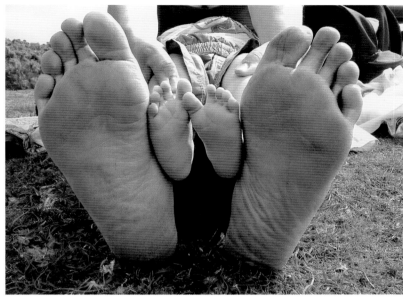

SWANSEA, SOUTH WALES *Proportion.* Neo Cooper, 5 months, sits in the lap of his mother, Karen, 31. 'We were sitting on the grass chatting,' Karen says. 'My eldest son, Luke, who is 10, suddenly noticed that baby Neo has my feet — even the little toe that curls under.' Luke snapped the picture.   Luke Cooper

AMATEURS

The *UK at Home* project invited talented amateurs to capture all the special moments that define home life and to submit them for possible inclusion in this book. Think of it as audience participation. More than 29,000 images were submitted by amateurs to the project website and a selection of their images, depicting UK home life in all its glory, are included on the following pages and interspersed throughout this book.

NOTTING HILL, LONDON *Last of the season.* Alice Marbach, 8, still in her school uniform, shows off the final potatoes of the year's harvest. 'There is nothing like harvesting potatoes from your garden,' says her mother Emily. 'You put your hand in the soil and you find these small white gems!' 📷 Emily Marbach

BRENTWOOD, ESSEX *Swing time.* Ellie Page, 7, poses on the swing in her family's back garden. 'This photograph perfectly captures Ellie's sense of fun,' says her dad, Richard. 'Both she and her brother Ben love playing in the garden.' 📷 Richard Page

ST LAWRENCE BAY, ESSEX *Twixt the two.* Sally and Robin Scagell pose in the doorway of one of their two homes. This one, a former oyster fisherman's cottage and once part of a Second World War POW camp, overlooks the Blackwater estuary. The other home stands high on a hill in the Chilterns. 'We hate to leave one for the other,' says Sally. 📷 Sally Scagell

BALLYNAHINCH, COUNTY DOWN *The Queen!* William and Evelyn Brown have decorated their home to match their extensive collection of Royal Family figurines and memorabilia. 'I have always been interested in the Royal Family,' says Evelyn. 'I think it began with Princess Margaret's wedding.' 📷 Ben Speck

HOME AND MEMORY

WHENEVER I HEAR THE WORD 'HOME', I think of the oak table in our dining room.

My parents worked as GPs, out early and back late, so during the week meals were rushed and casual — usually I would eat in the kitchen, on a high stool, or in the living room, plate on lap in front of the television. But at weekends we would eat together and then the table would come into its own, its grainy top so brightly polished that the panes of the sash windows were duplicated there, in miniature. In one corner there was a little dent, in the shape of a bird like a grebe or moorhen — a flaw in the wood, which I'd run my finger over, loving the texture.

The table meant warmth, solidity, durability. Gregariousness, too, especially at Christmas, when my cousins would drive over from Manchester to have lunch with us. Sometimes there would be as many as 15 for turkey and plum pudding, and an extra table would be put out, with us children forming a T at the far end. I'd gaze down the long oak table, the adults massed around it like Jesus's disciples at the Last Supper, and wonder if I'd ever grow up or marry or have children or live in such a house with such a table.

Now my parents are dead and the oak table stands in my dining room. We don't use it much, even for dinner parties: eating in the kitchen seems less bother. And though you can fit eight round it at a pinch, six is the most it will take comfortably. Not that it's shrunk, of course. But reality has — or, rather, the wide horizons of childhood turn out to be narrower than they seemed at the time. The table isn't just smaller but darker and more scratched than I remember it. And there are two dents on the surface, one of them bird-shaped (I got that much right), but neither in the corner. If somebody came along and told me that the table wasn't made of oak, but some other wood, I would not be altogether surprised. Even the sturdiest of memories turn out, when put to the test, to be flimsy.

My house is full of furniture my parents owned and which they, in turn, had inherited: wardrobes, dressers, chairs, desks, cupboards, tables. If my house is in a time-warp, that's partly because I'm too mean or lazy to go out looking for new stuff and partly, too, that I hate the values of our disposable culture, where nothing is deemed worth keeping (or mending) if it's more than five years old.

But the real reason behind my hoarding of objects is the memories that they provoke. They're not all good memories, nor can I rely on them being completely accurate. But they're part of who I am and what made me and of the story I carry round in my head.

So the oak table makes me think not just of Christmases with my cousins but of a particular lunch from which my mother, normally a stoic, fled in tears because of an anti-Irish joke made by my father (she being Irish and missing her family). The dangerously leaning wardrobe in our bedroom reminds me of the one that fell on my sister when she was nine (my mother had to drag her from underneath it). The rolltop desk at which I'm writing this stirs memories of my father's surgery and his disinclination to write prescriptions for patients he suspected of slacking ('Give them drugs and they'll be better in a week,' he used to say, 'give them nothing and it'll be seven days'). As for the shrivelled black wet suit hanging in the garage, I associate it with teenage summers when I used to water-ski.

Photographs are a more obvious way to prompt memory, and the chest of drawers in my study is crammed with albums that commemorate childhood and adolescence. But photos can be misleading. There's one of me, at 12, with a grass skirt, bikini top and hoola-hoop — I've no memory of why I was wearing the outfit but if the photo suggests a fondness for cross-dressing, or a future as a transvestite, these tendencies have been sadly unfulfilled.

Other photos I have show my mother smiling — an adored wife, proud parent and energetic career woman. She was all those things. But she could also be 'low' and unhappy for long periods, and I can remember an occasion when misery so got the better of her that she packed a suitcase and abruptly took off.

Do we ever really know the people we live with? Photos give us a face, but not what goes on behind it. 'That's caught him perfectly,' we say, but something always escapes capture and comprehension. I felt close to my mother. But she was an enigma. Only after her death, when I read the letters she had written during wartime, years before I was born, did I come to understand her.

We all rewrite the past as we get older, modifying this memory or that in the light of later experience. Once we're parents, for example, we are better placed to judge our own parents — to see where and why they went wrong, and to appreciate their strengths. When I was 13, my sister, two years behind me, failed her 11-plus exam. Believing the local secondary modern lacked the resources to provide her with a decent education, my parents sent her off to boarding school — but allowed me, already ensconced at the local grammar school, to remain at home. My sister endured an unhappy few years, feeling punished for her academic failure, before my parents, regretting their decision, brought her home again. Their mistake cast a shadow which never really faded. But even my sister never doubted that they loved her and were doing what they thought was best.

Home may be the source of our affections, but it is also the heart of the action — the site of life's most intense dramas and traumas. Some female novelists, including Jane Austen, have been chided for being too 'domestic'. But what's narrow about domesticity? Aren't the minutiae of family life of more lasting consequence than the great events of public life? Two-thirds of our life is spent at home. It's where we eat, sleep, wake, play, make love, raise children — and, increasingly, do our work. People used to be born and die at home, too, and in much of the world that's still the case. But nowadays most births and deaths in Western society take place away from home, anonymously, behind screens, in hospitals, as though life's most intimate and primal experiences were unmanageable without the intervention of professional outsiders. I was glad to be there for the deaths of my parents, just as I was for the births of my children. It felt natural. It felt right. It felt like a kind of homecoming, as well as a departure.

That's what home is: the place you keep coming back to, either in reality or in your dreams. Most of us have maps in our heads of the flats or houses we lived in as children: we know the layout of the rooms, the colour of the wallpaper, the view out the window, the bric à brac that sat on the mantelpiece. Most of the maps we consult in life are unfamiliar and require interpretation. But the map of our childhood home is permanently imprinted on the brain, and what went on there is embedded in our souls.

For me, now, writing this, home is a basement in south London. I'm below the ground, as if in a burrow, with a view out and upwards onto a back garden. It feels like a haven, in time as well as space — as I look out, there's nothing to tell me which year or even century this is. Life out there in the world is fraught, demanding, frenetic. In here I can withdraw, lie low, take stock and let my mind wander.

Where it wanders, almost inevitably, is to my other home, the one I grew up in, a stone rectory in the Pennines with a view of distant moors. At times the memories are exhilarating, at times they bring tears to my eyes. 'Home is so sad,' Philip Larkin wrote, 'a joyous shot at how things ought to be/Long fallen wide'.

I know what he means. There are objects around me — that oak table not least — which remind me that my parents are dead and that the marriage they had was far from perfect. But whose marriage is perfect? And whose life doesn't come to an end?

I know my childhood was more happy than unhappy and that my parents, whatever their failings, were decent people doing their best. And the hoarded objects that fill my current home confirm that, reconnecting me to lost time. That oak table might not be big enough to host a large dinner party. But I know if I stare long and hard enough the film of my past life will spool across it and the dead will flicker back to life. 🏠

Blake Morrison is a professor and the author of the memoir And When Did You Last See Your Father?

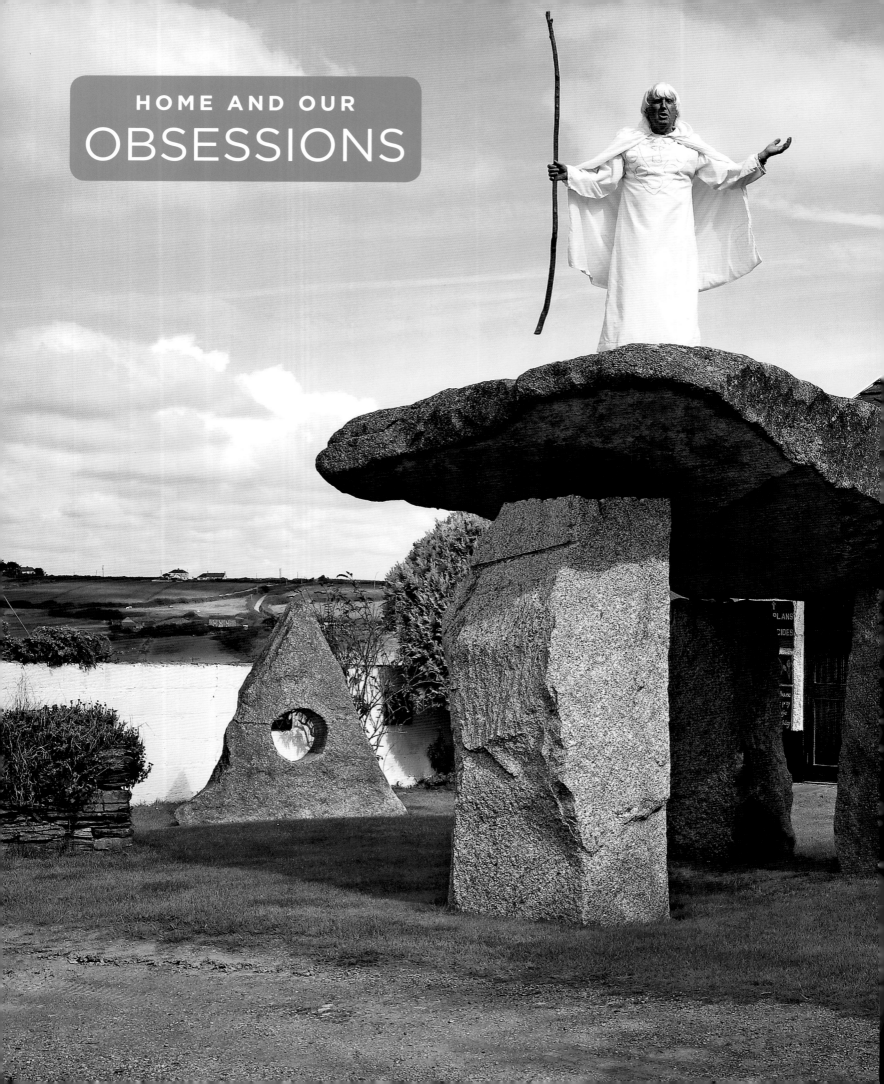

ST MERRYN, CORNWALL *Homehenge.* Edward Christopher Hambley Prynn, 71, is the self-proclaimed Archdruid of Cornwall. Since he was a child, he has been drawn by the power of standing stones. A quarry injury at the age of 32 set him on his life's work. Today there are 21 of these monoliths standing in the garden of his bungalow on the north coast of Cornwall. The first was erected in 1982 and the last in 1999. He is standing on The Angel's Runway, which weighs 18.5 tons. ◎ Simon Roberts

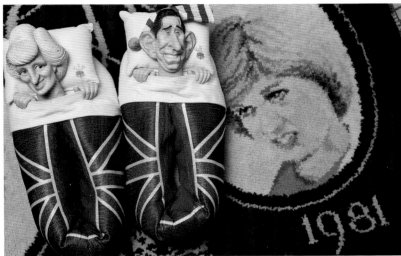

Bedtime. Margaret began filling her house with royal memorabilia 28 years ago. She named her eldest son after Prince Andrew and even moved to London at the age of 19 to be near the royals. Besides her collection, she also owns 1,600 books on the topic. 📷 Mike Goldwater

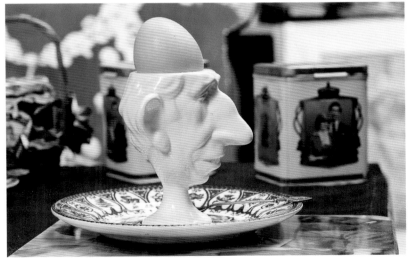

Egghead. Besides running her royalty-themed bed & breakfast, Margaret Tyler often finds herself being contacted by the world media to use her house and collection as a backdrop whenever there is a royal event. In that respect, she is living out her dream of being as close as possible to the monarchy. 📷 Mike Goldwater

ISLE OF SKYE *Sheep shape.* Vic Bull was recently offered £500,000 for his two-bedroom bungalow because of its extraordinary views of Loch Bay, but he turned the offer down. Vic moved to the island 14 years ago, when he bought, sight unseen, six acres of land with a cottage, a bungalow and three crofts. Today with the help of four dogs, he breeds Blackface sheep, Scotland's most common breed. Vic shows his 70 sheep twice a year — and the rosettes and ribbons on the wall of his house are testament to his success. 📷 Richard Baker

WHITWELL, ISLE OF WIGHT *Spoonfuls of memories.* Gloria Rolfe's mother and grandmother collected teaspoons as keepsakes from their travels — and Gloria, 67, continues the family tradition today. Her collection, now more than 250 spoons, is often added to by friends and family who bring them back from their journeys. 'I give my collection a clean once a year, in time for Christmas,' she says. 'Whenever I go anywhere, I have to have a memento of my time there.' 📷 Vicki Couchman

DADDRY SHIELDS, COUNTY DURHAM *Wave guide.* Dr Bob Coates has been collecting vintage radios for 20 years. He has nearly 400 models from all over the world — even Iceland — that he keeps in his garage. His wife, Mary, also 60, jokes that she may well divorce him and cite the radios as co-respondents. 📷 Justin Leighton

PWLLHELI, NORTH WEST WALES *Stuck on collecting.* Kathryn Ellis, 50, is a keen collector of Staffordshire pink china. She also owns nearly 700 hat pins, as well as collections of handkerchiefs and glass. Her mother was also a great collector and it all started for Kathryn when she was given three hat pins. She went to school and told her friends — and by the end of the week she had 30 hat pins from her friends' grandmothers. Her favourite is this one, with a picture of suffragette Emmeline Pankhurst on the top. 📷 Steve Peake

STEPNEY, LONDON *Familiar faces.* Standing at the creeper-wreathed gates of Todd Longstaffe Gowan and Tim Knox's house, it's hard not to feel like Pip visiting Miss Havisham. Todd is a gardener and historian and Tim is the director of the Sir John Soane's Museum. 'When we moved in 10 years ago no one had lived here for 100 years,' says Tim. They set up home in the gloom and took care in the restoration not to remove any of the original surfaces — or the original atmosphere. 📷 Barry Lewis

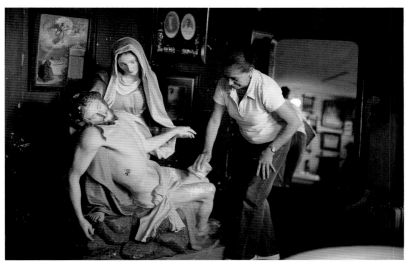

Sponge bath. Teresa De Las Casas has worked for Todd and Tim for five years and spends two days a week taking care of the hundreds of quirky antique artifacts around the house, including a death mask of Napoleon. 'Some collectors are purists about quality and collect only in narrow historical periods,' says Todd, 'but we rather like these mad arrangements.' Here Teresa cleans a pietà in the bathroom. 📷 Barry Lewis

HORDEN, COUNTY DURHAM *All aflutter.* Mervyn Wild, a life-long pigeon fancier, has 60 birds. He has lived in the same village all his life, met his wife in the village pub, and they have lived in the same house for 30 years. He spends six hours a day with his birds on his allotment. 'I let them out for a run twice a day for an hour each time. I've got a shed up there and me and my mates are always cracking on about pigeons.' 📷 Zak Waters

MALLUSK, COUNTY ANTRIM *Slurp.* When Stephen, 41, and Heather McMurray, 42, bought their house it was the local petrol station, post office and shop — there were still cans of beans and soup on the shelves. Now their house, which dates back to the 1700s, is also home to an ever-changing collection of rescued animals. With no official funding, their charity, 7th Heaven Animal Rescue Trust, relies on fundraising events and donations to keep going. Last year 7th Heaven re-housed 250 animals in kind and loving homes. 📷 Justin Kernoghan

ENSTONE, OXFORDSHIRE *Feline trouper.* For the past 11 years, Elizabeth Thornton, 39, has run the A1 animal talent agency from her home. Her four dogs and 14 cats have been in such films as *Cold Mountain, Snatch, Nanny McPhee* and *Children of Men,* as well as in numerous television dramas and advertisements. She describes herself as an animal lover 'in the extreme'. 📷 Mike Abrahams

CORWEN, NORTH WALES *Enraptored.* Lou Jones, 42, and her husband, Islwyn, 48, share their home with many pets including frequent visits from Jake, an American red-tail hawk. Islwyn says that without receiving regular attention the hawk, which is usually well behaved in the house, would be completely wild again in a week. 📷 Steve Peake

TREMADOG, GWYNEDD *Look homeward, angel.* Eric Jones, 70, was the first man to climb the north face of the Eiger alone — and was nearly killed in an avalanche. Today, still climbing, Eric runs a climbing school as well as a guest house. He also likes to jump — from planes, off skyscrapers and down mountainsides. 'I still get the tightness in my stomach before I jump and I've done it 492 times!' he says. One of Eric's favourite climbs is up this cliff directly above his own home. 📷 Steve Peake

"More young British people vote for TV's *Big Brother* programme than in political elections. Millions of people happily take part in telephone votes for TV but in the last general election, only 61 percent of voters turned out."

– Trevor Davis, *Citizenship in Modern Britain*

ELSTREE STUDIOS, HERTFORDSHIRE *Gobsmacked.* The first *Big Brother* TV show was broadcast in the Netherlands in September 1999. The first UK version aired in 2000. *Celebrity Big Brother* was introduced in 2003 and, between them, the shows — which typically feature at least 10 contestants confined under 24-hour camera coverage in a purpose-built house for two months — have caused their fair share of controversy. Here, members of the production staff rearrange the house at the end of the season. John Reardon

ORMEAU, BELFAST *A heart that's true.* A life-sized statue of Elvis sits above the bay window of 54-year-old Martin Rice's house. Martin's home is a tribute to Graceland and he has hundreds of costumes, posters, photographs and other Elvis memorabilia. When Presley died in 1977, Martin began turning his home into a shrine. At least once a week he dresses in costume and performs in schools, clubs or church halls for charity. Justin Kernoghan

HINCKLEY, LEICESTERSHIRE *Phasers on.* After eight years of work, designer Tony Alleyne recently finished converting his wife Georgina's flat into a precise, copy of *Star Trek*'s *Voyager* starship. He did all of the work except the plumbing. Since finishing, Tony has been contacted by photographers and cinematographers wanting to use the flat as a set. Tony, 54, who runs a company specialising in scientific design, is now working on his next project: a contemporary Laurence Llewelyn-Bowen-style creation. Thomas Brandi

SHOREDITCH, LONDON *Throwback.* 'I believe in romance and glamour,' says restorer and designer Johnny Vercoutre, 40. 'I spent six months wooing the most beautiful girl in the world — Miss Joy — with a Fifties Humber limo and vintage champagne.' As an art director for period films, Johnny specialises in historically correct motifs from the Forties and Fifties. The ground floor of his Georgian house, which he restored himself, is a Forties-style cinema, which he uses for private parties and screenings. 📷 Mary McCartney

WINDERMERE, LAKE DISTRICT *Sole full.* The rows of Wellingtons in the mud room of this home in Windermere speak volumes about the muck and sogginess of the surrounding countryside. The first Wellingtons made their appearance in 1817 and quickly caught on with patriotic English gentlemen as the perfect footwear for wet weather. The boots were manufactured in huge quantities during World War II and were particularly useful in 1944–45 for those troops assigned the task of clearing Holland of the enemy, who had to work in horrendous flooded conditions. By the time the war ended the Wellington had become popular throughout Britain among all ages and all classes. 📷 Rick Smolan

" The average Briton considers himself a good driver, possesses a copy of Queen's *Greatest Hits* and is 5 feet 9 inches tall, 40 years old and has a 37–inch waist. "

– Tim Wardle, *In Search of Mr Average*

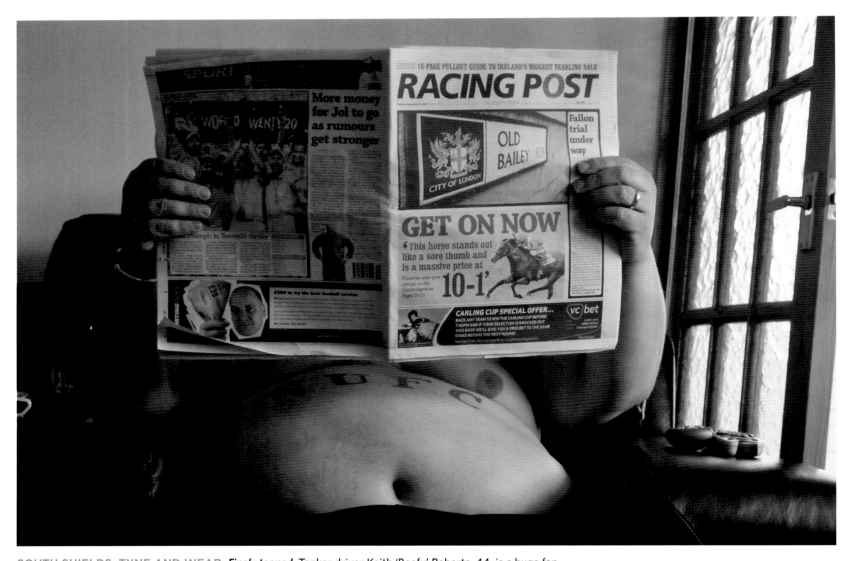

SOUTH SHIELDS, TYNE AND WEAR *Finely tooned.* Tanker driver Keith 'Beefy' Roberts, 44, is a huge fan of Newcastle United — so much so that he had NUFC tattooed on his stomach in 1999 before the team played Roma. 'My friends joked about my fat belly, so I thought I should make good use of it,' Keith says. Recently, he lost five stone, threatening his living billboard, but luckily 'it came off everywhere but my belly'. Zak Waters

HAYWARDS HEATH, WEST SUSSEX *Sedan chair.* Johnny Woodford, 45, sculptor and woodworker, catches up with the news on his 'Sedan Sh****r' — a composting toilet with handles for easy relocation. Johnny owns and lives on six acres of woodland in the Sussex countryside, where he builds alternative living structures and sculptures. 📷 Roger Bamber

Crux of the matter. Johnny, 45, is a noted sculptor and woodworker who specialises in creating alternative living options. He has found his spiritual home in six acres of field and woodlands in Sussex and is now working to turn it into the burial site for himself, his friends and family. 'I never tire of this place,' he says, 'and hope to one day dive into the earth here for ever.' 📷 Roger Bamber

Submerged. Never without his hat, even indoors, Johnny takes a bath, which he gets to through a trap door in the floor and which is heated by the wood-burning stove. Johnny's home is a comfortable wooden 'Ark' that he built himself on the base of an old fairground trailer. 📷 Roger Bamber

JACKIE KAY

THE UNLIKELY HOME

KEYS

Round your neck, a string with a Yale and a Chubb, the key to your front door maybe, back door, garage. The key to your chicken coop, rabbit hutch, bicycle padlock. The key to your past, future, marriage. The key to your carriage. The key to knowledge. Sometimes, in some houses, through the various addresses that will build up the story of your life, when you've been furnished with keys in different places, when your hands have played the key board and your ears have listened to the key notes, and you've keyed in all the information, and you are all keyed up, sometimes you might just want to throw away the key. Sometimes you wish someone held the small gold key to your heart.

I had my own key to my house, 183 Brackenbrae Avenue, Bishopbriggs, Glasgow by the time I was ten. It made me feel grown up. At lunchtimes I could open the door to my empty house and experience that particular eerie quiet of a house without its people, my parents and my brother. I remember noticing how familiar and yet unfamiliar the house felt then, on those odd lunch hours, almost as if you could hear the house breathing. Sometimes my pal Jenny Harvey would come back with me and we would heat up a tin of spaghetti Bolognese and play my dad's jazz and blues records. Bessie Smith, Pearl Bailey, Ma Rainey.

I had the key to our house round my neck on a piece of string. Both my best friends had their own key to their houses, usually just to the front door. But the keys my brother and I were furnished with were very different.

I was a black child in a white neighbourhood; but inside my house I felt safe and at home. I was adopted as a baby and always felt like I belonged to my mum and dad. They were bright, enthusiastic, entertaining, protective, loyal and loving parents. A Wimpey house in suburban Glasgow perhaps seemed an unlikely place for me to find such love. But there it was, an ordinary house whose very garden path and four walls were made extraordinary and special because of the people inside the house.

I was lucky. I felt my place was with my adoptive parents; I

naturally fitted and suited them. I felt so strongly at home that I imagined if I had ever been up in the sky and had the chance to look down on a particular parental orchard, I would have hand picked my parents from the trees there.

Outside the warmth and humour of our particular house, the neighbourhood was less likely. After my mum adopted my brother, also black, she had a visit from the local minister, who wanted to tell her what a kind act of God she had done in bringing native children into her house. My parents set off a whole spate of adoption in the neighbourhood. My mum was always having cups of tea and giving advice to other would-be adoptive parents who wanted to bring unlikely children into likable homes.

But like I said, I was lucky. Some of my friends who were not adopted, who shared their mother's eyes and their father's nose, their mother's hands and father's feet, found themselves not at home in their own home.

JENNY AND THE GARDEN PATH

You might have been led up or down the garden path. Or you took the wrong path. Where you once stood there was another path. You lost your way — for a while you were pathless. Or you stood at the crossroad and took the road less travelled, the path less trodden. There once was a pathway clear as day to your future. Then all of a sudden, it was a steep cliff path, it was the path down to the sea. You and I were on the same path for a while. Then you were knocked off your path. Now it seems you would like someone to find a pathway to your brain.

My good pal Jenny wasn't happy, like the rest of us, when the school bell went. She walked home slowly. Her house was actually too near the school. She would have relished a long walk home — the longer the walk the better, the less time she would have to spend inside her house. She never knew what to expect when she was coming up the garden path. Her feet in her black school shoes felt heavy. The garden path was overgrown. The garden gate had a strange creak; every time she heard it, she remembered that everything she dreaded began with that noise.

The phone was on the hall table but the phone was cut off. Jenny couldn't ring any friends; she couldn't ring me. We wished we lived nearer so that we could have Morse code. We wished we could be like children in a Secret Seven novel and have pitchers of homemade lemonade and homemade ginger biscuits.

You'd go into Jenny's house and already sense trouble. There was the silent phone in the hall, the cigarette smoking itself in the ashtray, the house already dark in the afternoon, the mum mostly gone. Her mum was sometimes there and sometimes in the mental hospital. Jenny never talked about her mum's strange absences; she was perhaps frightened of them, as if they were lying up ahead, waiting for her when she got older. She was left with her drinking, smoking dad whose tall edgy energy created a thick atmosphere in her house. We would go to her box bedroom where she had an old gramophone, and there we'd play and mime to songs by blues women. Jenny had a great jazz voice and fabulously arched eyebrows, and great style — even when she was 10 years old. The music contained and entertained her. It was as if Jenny was reaching out for another possible life — one where she could dance and sing, and belong to another time and family altogether.

The last time I saw Jenny she was eating 14 bars of raisin and biscuit Yorkies a day and drinking several pints of cider mixed with lager to form Snakebites. I kept thinking of the girl who loved to dance; where she'd gone.

KENNETH AND THE ROOF TOP

When you were small you wanted to raise the roof. You wanted more from life than a roof over your head. You'd love to have stood on some high plateau in another country altogether, to spread your arms out on the roof of the world and have the sun shine down on you. Before you escaped your childhood home, the roof of your mouth was often dry with fear. The only respite at home was to climb up into the small roof garden and look out on the roofs of the world, the red roofs and slate roofs and thatched roofs, the brick and stone roofs, the corrugated iron roofs and car roofs and roof racks, and know that one day you would go through one roof, skip over another roof, and land like a cat on a hot tin roof in another life entirely.

My pal Kenneth knew he was gay from a very early age and told his mother and father. They were both members of an idiosyncratic and peculiar religious sect, the Wee Free. His father told Kenneth that

homosexuality was an abomination. Their marriage had been dictated by the church, in the tiny Scottish island they hailed from, and there was no happiness in it.

Kenneth said he felt like he didn't belong to either of them. He called his parents Him and Boo. He gave his mother the name Boo because she was so easily scared. 'Him says I can't come out tonight,' Kenneth would say.

If Kenneth angered his father, in any silly way, just by questioning something he said, he would be locked in the cupboard under the stairs until he broke down and begged to be let out. His mother was a kind woman that Kenneth loved, but she too was afraid of 'Him's' rages, how he would suddenly fly off the handle and smash plates in the kitchen.

Kenneth told me that he used to be able to stay under the stair cupboard for the longest time. He would listen to the sound of feet on the stairs. In a way, he would feel safe under there with the coats and the Hoover and the Wellington boots. When he was inside the dark cupboard under the stairs he would imagine himself up high in a roof garden with beautiful bright flowers growing.

Not all of my friends had unhappy homes, but those that did made a huge impression on me. I never forgot the feeling of the unhappy home. As a child, I imagined that the house itself was unhappy — filled to the rafters with sad people — so that the stone the house was made of could soak up sadness. I imagined that each room in the home of an unhappy family somehow matched the family's sorrow. I could put up yellow wallpaper in the rooms of such houses: the house of cards, the house of games, the house of Bernarda Alba. My mum would always say, 'Nobody knows what goes on behind four walls.'

The walls in the happy house create rooms, roomy rooms. The thick, silent walls in the sad house close in like winter nights.

It is only love that makes the walls and mirrors of a house glow and only love that lets the sunlight stream through the windows; only love that makes you want to sing from the red rooftops, raise a glass and raise the glass ceiling; love that makes a song and dance, love that says that you are home. 🏠

Jackie Kay is the author of the poetry collection The Adoption Papers *and the novel* Trumpet.

HOME AND OUR COMPANIONS

SHOREDITCH, LONDON *Fairy Tales*. Sisters Tinky and Twinkle Troughton, members of the punk band, The Fairies, pose tough but play nice. Known throughout London for randomly granting wishes to strangers, the pair and two other band mates, Tinsel and Sparkle, sport fairy wings on (and off) stage. 'We wore fairy wings to a party a few years ago and decided not to take them off,' says Twinkle. The only restrictions they place on wishes is that 'when we grant men a wish, it can't be about a Fairy herself,' says Twinkle. 🔟 Jo Broughton

LODSWORTH, WEST SUSSEX *Against the grain.* For 10 years, Ben Law, author
of *The Woodland House*, lived in tents and caravans. Finally, after a lengthy planning
battle, he was given permission to build a house — which he did by hand, with help from
volunteers, using the materials growing around him. The finished house was built with an
A-frame made of tree trunks, a wooden floor and sweet chestnut roof shingles. 'I belong
here,' Ben says. 'When I am here everything in the world is all right.' 📷 Charlie Gray

" A family is a unit composed not only of children but of men, women, an occasional animal, and the common cold. "

– Ogden Nash

Taste test. Kit and Kiki share some delicious cake mixture before cooking. 'We go to the park and to messy play-days at the local library,' says Kit. 'I think at first there were some raised eyebrows because generally I was the only guy. But once the other mums saw how I interacted with Kiki, I think everyone found it much more normal. We spend a lot of the day playing — she's quite a bundle of energy.' 📷 Vicki Couchman

Spring form. Kit bakes with his daughter Kiki. Between jobs, Kit has spent most of the past year as Kiki's primary carer. 'It's been incredibly rewarding,' he says. 'Kiki's independent, stubborn and quite rough-and-tumble for a girl.' 📷 Vicki Couchman

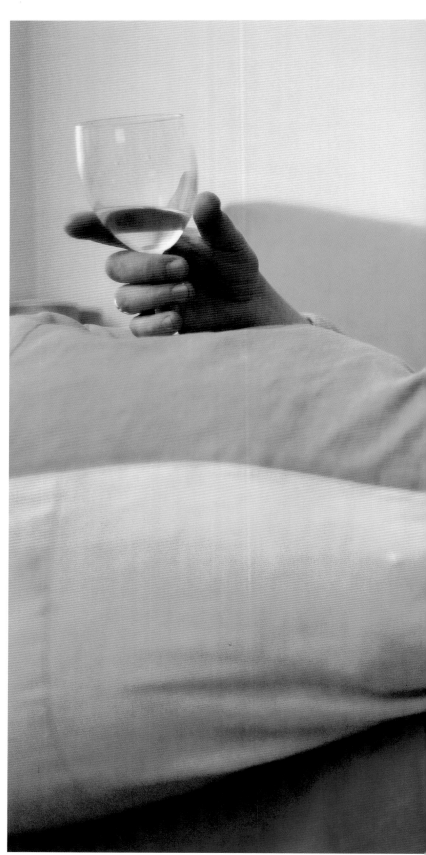

> " As one grows older, one becomes wiser and more foolish. "
>
> – François de la Rochefoucauld

LIVINGSTON, WEST LOTHIAN *Bouncing back.* Liz McNamee, 30, and her fiancé, Stuart Mackenzie, 39, met online through a dating agency. 'We spoke by phone, decided to meet up and hit it off,' Liz says. 'I just knew that was it for the rest of my life and he felt the same.' Now pregnant with twins, Liz already had three children when she met Stuart: Alistair, 11, Jamie, 9, and Katie, 4. The twinning rate in the UK has increased by around 50% in the past 20 years, with the rise attributed to an increase in maternal age, wider use of IVF and assisted conception and the advancement of medical technology. 📷 Cecilia Magill

TAUNTON, SOMERSET *Family pastoral.* For the past five years Martine Croenen, 37, and Andy Borgiis, 40, have lived on a permanent caravan site with 10 pitches occupied by other families and individuals. Their daughter, Meriden, 4, recently started in reception at the local school. 'Living like this is so much more community-oriented,' says Martine. 'There are a lot of children here varying in age from one to about 16. They all get on well and there's lots of space for them to play and explore.' 📷 David Partner

CANVEY ISLAND, ESSEX *Our little haven.* Lynne O'Connor, 49, has lived in her council flat for 10 years and she sees it as her refuge. She's had a difficult life but when she's at home with her son Zak, 6, she feels safe. Every wall of their house is covered with memories. In the corner of the lounge Lynne keeps mementos and pictures of her daughter, who died two years ago. 📷 Duncan Raban

DAGENHAM, ESSEX *Down time.* Mani, 14, Akelah, 16, and Emanuel Brenton, 10, play a game on the computer together. Their father, Ras, is a firm believer in the Rastafari movement and the family often travels to Ethiopia, the heart of Rastafarianism. 'Our home is not just a place to physically rest but also a spiritual place,' Ras says. 'It's a place to escape from the trials and tribulations of the outside and find comfort and security.'   Pål Hansen

[Nearly 15 million households in Great Britain (more than 60 percent) now have access to the Internet. This is an increase of more than 25 percent in just four years.]

HACKNEY, LONDON *Key word.* Madeleine Waller, 40, an artist specialising in portraits, and Louis Modell, her son, aged 10, are using the Internet to look up a history timeline for Louis's homework. As with many families, the Internet has become a constant resource for homework in their household. David Modell

[Trends in birth, death and migration have led to an ageing of UK's population.
Of the 62 million people living in the UK today, approximately 17 percent are 65 or older.]

BEDWORTH, WARWICKSHIRE *Close relatives.* Cousins Joan Thompson, 86, and Joan Francis, 85, grew up in the same neighbourhood outside Coventry and spent most of their childhood together until they were sent off to different schools. They drifted apart and didn't really see each other for the next 70 years. Recently reunited, they now live in the Richmond Villages retirement home and spend more time with each other than with anyone else. Says Joan Francis, 'It's lovely company having Joan here.' David Levene

WHITWELL, ISLE OF WIGHT *Home from home.* Kiki Lett, almost 3, lives in London with her parents, but stays with her grandparents on the Isle of Wight every couple of months, when her mother's work takes her overseas. 'We treat her like we did our three children,' says her grandmother, Beryl Couchman, 73. In the UK, 60% of childcare is provided by grandparents, and one in every 100 children is living with a grandparent. 📷 Vicki Couchman

CAPEL CURIG, CONWY, NORTH WALES *Superhero.* Lady Alice Douglas is the daughter of the Marquis of Queensbury, a title held by a member of the Douglas family since it was created in 1682. Here, Lady Alice and her daughter, Hero, practise a fire drill on the roof of their home, although it is more of a game than a serious activity. Their home is a converted church that Lady Alice bought and renovated. 📷 Roger Hutchings

Current trends indicate that by 2030 more than 25 percent of women will be the main breadwinner in UK households.

FORRES, MORAYSHIRE *Close scrape.* A sunny day in September seemed the perfect time for Veerle Van den Eynden, 39, to scrub down their 100-year-old oversized shed in preparation for painting the next day. 'The kids reckoned that anything involving ladders, heights and mucky water had to be fun, and joined me on the roof to help,' says Veerle of her children Joachim, 9, and Kaitlin, 7. 📷 Nicholas Snow

[The first item British homeowners would grab in the case of a fire or
other emergency would be the family photo album.]

PECKHAM, LONDON *Framed.* Attracted by the opportunity of a better life, 80-year-old retired nurse Loretta
Rodgers came to England from Jamaica in 1962 to join her husband. An average of 20,000 Jamaicans migrated
each year to the UK in the mid-1950s and early 1960s, swelling the Caribbean UK community to more than
900,000 people. But by 1994, a mere 300 Jamaicans emigrated to the UK. In 2006, more than 3,000 British
nationals emigrated back to Jamaica. Franklyn Rodgers

SINDLESHAM, BERKSHIRE *Survivor.* William 'Bill' Stone, 107, is one of five remaining British veterans from the First World War, and one of only two who also fought in the 1939–45 war. Behind him in his nursing home bedroom are flowers from his recent birthday, a card from the Queen and photographs of Bill with members of the Royal Family, leading politicians including Tony Blair, and other centenarian veterans. 📷 Edmund Clark

[Young women tend to leave the nest sooner than their male counterparts. Approximately 38 percent of 20 to 24-year-old women continue to live at home with their parents vs. 57 percent of men the same age.]

ABERGAVENNY, MONMOUTHSHIRE *Migrant student.* Living in Wales, Tara Pinnock, 10, crosses the border twice a day to go to school in England at the Hereford Waldorf School, with her brother Kailash. Waldorf (or Steiner) education is based on the educational philosophy of Rudolf Steiner, and emphasises the role of imagination and creativity in education. It's where Tara knitted the hat she is trying on. Tara and her family live in a fourteenth-century keep-house and barn, nestled into the side of a cliff in the Black Mountains.　📷 John Downing

CROUCH END, LONDON *Party prep.* Julia Cummings struggles to fix her false eyelashes as she prepares for her 18th birthday night out in sister Katy's bedroom. Rebecca Stone and Roberta Brandes get ready in the background. 'Becky and I have been best friends for about five years,' says Julia. 'Katy's at university quite a lot of the time now. Roberta is also at my school, so I've known her for nearly 11 years.' 📷 Barry Lewis

CROUCH END, LONDON *Bonding.* It's Rebecca's eighteenth as well today. Here she holds Julia's freshly glued eyelashes in place while she chats about party plans on her mobile. Julia's sister Katy, 21, right, gets ready to check herself in the mirror. 📷 Barry Lewis

LIVERPOOL, MERSEYSIDE *Reading and riding.* Liverpool boasts the oldest Chinese community in Western Europe. Chih Kao 'San' Tseng, 82, born in the Sichuan province, came to the UK in 1945, having joined the navy during the war. He settled in Liverpool, married an Englishwoman, and has lived here ever since. Sophia Campbell, 4, the youngest of his nine grandchildren, visits him every day. Although China is where his roots are, San says that Liverpool is his home. 📷 Andrew Buurman

BRIGHTON, EAST SUSSEX *Here's looking at you.* Johanna Berger, 40 (left), met Nic Compton, 44, nine years ago in Portugal. They remained friends and when she and her partner, Sonya Smith, 33, decided to have a baby, they asked Nic to be the father. Their daughter, Maia, is now three months old. Nic, who has two other children, visits regularly and thinks of himself as a part-time daddy. 📷 Mischa Haller

ABINGDON, OXFORDSHIRE *Together forever.* Debbie Robinson, 48, remembers being so exhausted during labour that she curled in a foetal position and silently asked her unborn daughter to push herself out. That's exactly what Ciara, now 12, did. After her birth, the two spent the next six hours asleep side by side — a tradition that continues to this day. No matter where they travel together, they still find home wrapped up in each other's arms. 📷 Rick Smolan

> " The best way to make children good is to make them happy. "
>
> – Oscar Wilde

HARINGAY, LONDON *Pat-a-cake.* Emila Wesowslska, 7, and her sister Sylvia, 9, take some time to play after school before starting their homework. The girls are the children of Polish Roma (gypsy) refugees who came with their family to north London. They have a younger brother, and another sibling on the way. Sylvia was born in Poland, Emila in England. According to the Home Office, 450,000 Poles and citizens of the seven other new EU states have applied to work in the UK since 2004. ◉ Gideon Mendel

TWICKENHAM, LONDON *Leaving their mark.* Leigh and Charlotte Bowen's house is a model of energy efficiency. Leigh, 34 and an architect, has converted this 1960s town house to be as efficient as possible, with solar heating and plumbing. It also has a fully automated wood pellet system that burns wood waste without smoke. Here the couple and their children, Phoebe, 3, and Nesta, three months, visit their nearly finished home. ◉ Dario Mitidieri

The average person in the UK will drink 80,000 cups of tea and consume 35,000 biscuits during his or her lifetime.]

GORING-BY-SEA, WEST SUSSEX *Loving care.* 'Henry is like an adopted father for us,' says Brenda Goodwin. Henry Allingham, 111, is the UK and Europe's oldest man. Henry grew up in east London and joined the Royal Naval Air Service in World War I. Married for 51 years, he has two daughters, six grandchildren, 12 great-grandchildren, 13 great-great-grandchildren and one great-great-great-grandchild. Henry lives in a home for blind ex-servicemen, but spends much of his time with Brenda and her husband, Dennis, who have looked after him for the past decade. 📷 Edmund Clark

ORMSKIRK, LANCASHIRE *Grand auntie.* Flo Kane, 88, plays with her great-grand-niece, seven-month-old Bryony. Nearby stand sisters Barbara Yates, 65 (Bryony's grandmother), and Pauline Halliday, 82. Barbara, Pauline and their husbands pooled their money 20 years ago to buy this house together — and it has become a gathering place for the extended family. 'Because there are so many of us, the house has always been full of lots of people,' says Barbara. 📷 Andrew Buurman

NEW CROSS, LONDON *Remember when?* Loretta Rodgers, 80, and Dorell James, 75, both emigrated to the UK from Jamaica in the early Sixties. They also worked as auxiliary nurses on the geriatric ward at Greenwich District Hospital until they retired. These days they like to get together at Loretta's home in New Cross and reminisce about old times. 📷 Franklyn Rodgers

" If you cannot get rid of the family skeleton, you may as well make it dance. "

–George Bernard Shaw

WOKING, SURREY *Passing time.* The UK has one of the highest rates of incarceration in Western Europe and women represent about 6% of all prison inmates. Here, Terry Williams (right), 49, in for six years for conspiracy to steal, and Paris Kuedorvitch, 29, serving a six-year sentence for importing drugs, spend some time together at HMP Send. 'Terry's like a mum to me,' says Paris, 'someone I can always go to. We hug a lot and cry together when it gets too much.' HMP Send is a training prison, offering inmates access to education and vocational training courses.　📷 Edmund Clark

MIDDLEWICH, CHESHIRE *Kin folk.* Liz Rosenfield (third from left) and her husband Ian Murfitt (standing, right) live in a house filled with dogs, children and musical instruments. Liz, a special needs teacher, organises the annual Middlewich Folk and Boat Festival. The rest of the year, friends, family — between them, they have five children from previous marriages — musicians, and even visitors passing through on boats, regularly gather at their house to play music. 📷 Ivor Prickett

BISLEY, GLOUCESTERSHIRE *Framework.* Russ Dutton, 42, a landscape gardener and drystone waller, was born and brought up in the Cotswold village of Bisley. Three years ago, he, his wife Ness, 39, and their two boys moved into the house of their dreams: a beautiful, sixteenth-century stone cottage. 'The village is very dear to my husband,' says Ness, 'and we're here to stay.' 📷 John Downing

ORFORD, SUFFOLK *Day tripper.* Tamarisk Mitchell-Cotts, 8, pedals off from her new home to the village shops in nearby Orford. There were no shops near the family's former home in a remote coastal village so trips to buy penny sweets are a novelty — and a favourite pastime — for Tamarisk and her five siblings. 📷 Caroline Irby

> " The average Briton will say 'sorry' 1.9 million times in his life, spend one month of his life looking for lost socks and spend 45 hours a year 'on hold' on the telephone. He will go on a foreign holiday once a year. "

– Tim Wardle, *In Search of Mr Average*

WHITWELL, ISLE OF WIGHT *Recovery.* An exhausted Peter Couchman, 78, takes an afternoon nap, having spent the morning tending to his young granddaughter, Kiki Honey Mei Lett. 'We look after Kiki when her mum has to work away,' he says of himself and wife Beryl, 73. 'We love it but it is both tying and trying, because we are well past our spring chicken days. But it doesn't matter — all our friends are as in love with her as we are. We really are delighted to have her.' ◉ Vicki Couchman

MILDENHALL, WILTSHIRE *Profile.* Former journalist Michael Kallenbach, 58, moved to his home — composed of three small cottages knocked through — seven years ago. Now studying to be a psychotherapist, he also edits the local church newsletter (despite being Jewish). Michael has been with his partner, Robert Taylor, for 23 years. Last year they sealed their relationship with a civil partnership. The Civil Partnership Act came into force in December 2004 with almost 2,000 partnerships registered during that first month. 📷 Mike Abrahams

UPTON PARK, LONDON *Stepping out.* Older people are making up an increasing proportion of England's population. In the London Borough of Newham, the Eastwards Trust has been working for several years to meet the housing, health and social needs of elders in the Asian immigrant community. Its Hamara Ghar project is the largest sheltered housing scheme of its kind in the UK. Here a group of residents and friends including Prem Rani, 66, Kandimathi Sellathurai, 68, Bhanumathi Roa, 75, and Noor Reeds, 65, dance to Caribbean soca music for exercise and fitness. ◘ Kalpesh Lathigra

[Since the late 1990s migration into the UK has been an increasingly important
factor in UK population change. One big impact: during an average weekend one fifth
of everyone living in Britain will eat a curry.]

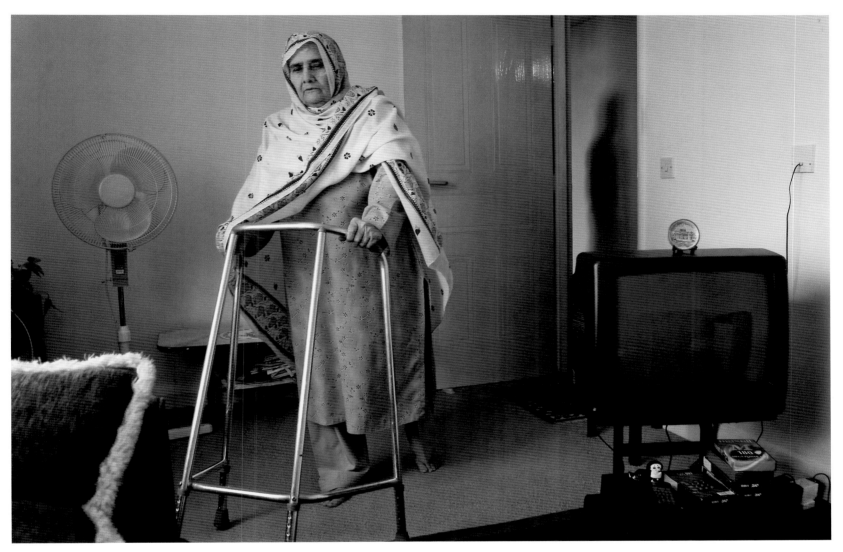

Strong support. Jamila Khwaja, 68, has lived at Hamara Ghar, a government-funded sheltered housing scheme
for elderly people from ethnic communities, since 1995. She moved to East Ham some years before from
Pakistan with her husband, Mohammed Aslam Khwaja, so they could be closer to their two daughters. Hamara
Ghar, which means 'my home' in Hindi, is run by a trust offering a number of community services to the elderly.
Jamila spends a lot of her time reading the Koran and, while she does the cooking, her husband does all the
shopping. 📷 Kalpesh Lathigra

TIDWORTH, HAMPSHIRE *Homecoming.* Abigail, 11, waits with her mum, Lindsey, 39, at the Aliwal Barracks for her father to arrive home after a five-month deployment in Iraq. Her dad, Kevin, 38, is a sergeant major and was travelling with 220 soldiers from the King's Royal Hussars Regiment, the first of 500 troops to be withdrawn from Iraq. 'I'm glad to be home,' says Kevin, 'but some of my thoughts are with the soldiers we left behind, and I will not completely relax until they are also all safely home.' ◎ Dario Mitidieri

Family reunion. Craig, 24, a trooper with the King's Royal Hussars, hasn't seen his baby daughter Ellie for four months, since he was posted to Iraq when she was just four weeks old. As the son of a fellow soldier looks on, Ellie gets a long-postponed kiss from her father. 'I was so pleased to come back and to be reunited with my wife and daughter,' says Craig. 'I was amazed by how much she had grown since I'd deployed.' 📷 Dario Mitidieri

BURY ST EDMUNDS, SUFFOLK *Across the generations.* Edna Hambling, 96, here talking to nurse Lizzie Featherstone, 21, lives in a retirement home run by the Royal Agricultural Benevolent Institution. The RABI was set up in 1860 as a charity for those in need in the farming community. It has two facilities: this one in Suffolk and the other in Somerset. The farming community is a small world and residents often know each other from their earlier lives or have had other relatives live in the home. 📷 Charlie Gray

BASILDON, ESSEX *Warm embrace.* Nine-month-old Ruby Walsh has severe cerebral palsy. Her mother, Charlotte, 26, used to be a youth worker but now cares full-time for her 'gorgeous' baby. Ruby is unlikely ever to be able to walk or talk, and Charlotte is grateful for the support she has. 'I get a lot from the hospice,' she says. 'Also from my husband Colin and my son Jack. And my mum is brilliant with helping out.' 📷 Mary McCartney

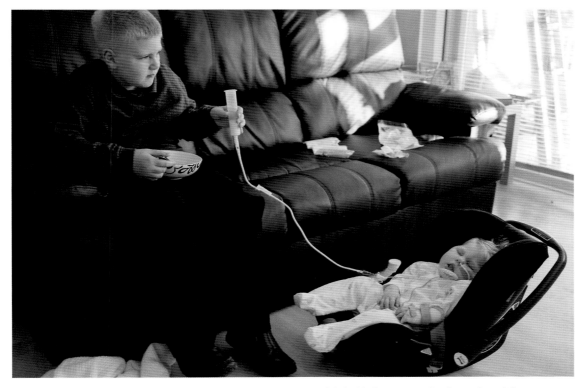

BASILDON, ESSEX *All together now.* Eight-year-old Jack Walsh holds his sister's feeding tube while eating breakfast and watching television. Ruby, nine months, has severe cerebral palsy. 'Jack is a gentle, kind, thoughtful boy,' says his mum, Charlotte. 'It can be hard, dividing time between the two, making sure Jack feel he's also getting some attention. He and I once managed to watch an entire episode of *Doctor Who* without interruptions — it was a blessing.' 📷 Mary McCartney

DORCHESTER, DORSET *Twists and turns.* Weekend guests look down from the musicians' balcony in a secluded estate house adorned with artwork and trappings which echo their owners' polyglot origins. Dorchester is famous as the home of the novelist Thomas Hardy who used the town as the setting for *The Mayor of Casterbridge,* as well as *Far from the Madding Crowd, Jude the Obscure* and *The Return of the Native.* 📷 Rick Smolan

STOCKPORT, GREATER MANCHESTER *Princess.* 'Mummy puts make-up on me and I look dead nice,' says 6-year-old Emily Kenny. 'When I grow up I would like to be a model or a teacher.' Emily lives with her postman father Sean Kenny, 39, and salesperson mother, Nicola, 31. Sean's workday ends at about noon, so he picks Emily up from school, and often cooks dinner. Nicola likes to spend her time with Emily playing dress-up, complete with eye shadow and nail varnish.   📷 Louis Quail

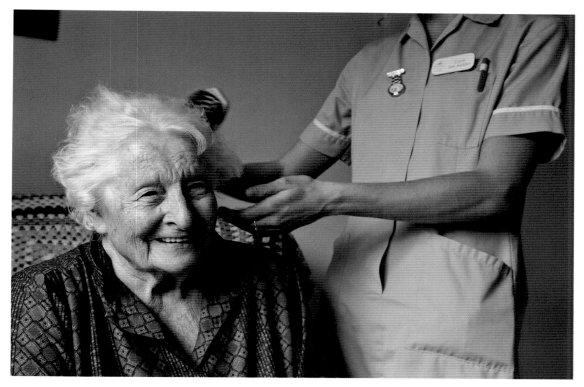

BURY ST EDMUNDS, SUFFOLK *Shampoo and set.* A farmer's wife since 1938, Janet Stamper, 91, is enjoying her later years in the Manson House retirement home. 'For my 80th birthday, I had a big surprise,' she remembers. 'I was taken to a nearby field — and a trailer turned up with a hot-air balloon on it! My son James and daughter Margaret came along too. I wasn't scared at all. We landed in a field where I knew the farmer's wife — she couldn't believe it was me!' Charlie Gray

KENTISH TOWN, LONDON *Glide.* Petra Mitidieri, 43, a mother of two, gets some grooming assistance from her 3-year-old daughter Mara. With a PhD in mechanical engineering, Petra consults clients on engineering challenges such as making ball bearings more efficient. As if that wasn't enough, she is also a qualified Ashtanga yoga instructor and teaches more than 20 classes each week. No matter how busy she gets, Petra always makes time for Mara and her 16-month-old son Nico. Dario Mitidieri

LLANRHAEADR, DENBIGHSHIRE *Lingering look.* Betty Jones, 66, studies a photograph of herself and her husband Dennis taken a few weeks before he died. The couple were married for 45 years and had one son. Dennis lived in the same house, left to him by his grandmother, for all of his 72 years. A beloved local plumber, who charged pensioners only £5 for his work, Dennis was honoured, in this village of 700 people, by 350 cards of condolence — too many for Betty to put them all up. 📷 Steve Peake

ROTHWELL, LEEDS, WEST YORKSHIRE *Ever green.* Jane Tomlinson used to joke that their garden should be turned into a football pitch after she died because her husband was such a poor gardener. Between her diagnosis at 26 with breast cancer in 1990 and her death in 2007, Jane famously took on a series of incredible physical challenges, including an Ironman Triathlon (the only person with incurable cancer ever to do so) and a bike ride across America. In the process, she raised £1.5 million for cancer charities and was awarded an MBE and a CBE. Her husband Mike Tomlinson tends their garden daily in her memory. 📷 Jocelyn Bain Hogg

LEAVING HOME

When I was sixteen I had to leave home.

As I set off down the gloomy hallway, past the coats hung like dead men, and the coin-slot gas meter that ticked and glowed like a golem, my mother called out to me. I turned, wondering if there would be some regret or a kind word. She said, 'Jeanette, why be happy when you could be normal?'

My mother, if she had known it, had asked me a question as wise, complex, and potentially fatal, as any fairy tale riddle, where the right answer leads to the treasure or the princess, and the wrong answer is Death by Ogre.

I had made the mistake of confessing first love, love that when requited makes us insanely happy. Unfortunately my love object was a girl and my family were strict evangelical Christians. And thus my mother's question… but it was really a question about life: life choices, life savers and life lines. It was not a question about lifestyle.

There is no such thing.

My family home was poor, and I took nothing with me because I had nothing to take. For the next couple of years I lived where I could, sometimes in the back of a car, sometimes in a tent, and finally in a boxroom lent to me by a teacher — I was still at school.

Trying to get to sleep in the back of a steamed-up car, I thought a lot about my mother's question. It wasn't a true opposition, like hot and cold, dark and light, and in any case, I wasn't so happy now that I was sleeping in a duffle coat in a Hillman Imp. I realised that while living by other people's rules is no guarantee of personal happiness, living outside of those rules is no Wonderland either. Happy/normal was going to take a lot of unpacking, and while I was heaving ideas around in my head, I had to deal with the pressing practical question of how to make something like a home in temporary, transient, unlikely and uncomfortable places.

It's a predicament that more and more people find themselves in, as life becomes less and less stable. That old fundamental, a happy home, is something we all want, but how do we make it happen?

And is it possible to create a happy home, even when you yourself are unhappy?

I only know of one way to begin — and it holds for the beautiful apartment, the nasty rented room, the bed-sit, the soulless little flat, the house you find yourself left with when the person you loved has gone, the place you take on because you have to get away, the nowhere-land, the transit zone.

I call it *Private Magic.*

When I was a child, a hearth rug was a flying carpet. Remembering this, in my borrowed room, I saved up some money from weekend work and bought myself a rug the size of a duster, one that folded into my case as easily as it expanded in my imagination. From then on, wherever I found myself, even in a doorway, I put down my little rug, and I began to feel calm. Better than calm, I imagined myself free. My rug became my comforter.

Years later, when I was awkwardly accepting a six-month stay at a rich man's house, I rolled up his Persian carpet in my room, and put down my own threadbare Arabian night. Rich or poor, I believe that you have to begin with one single thing that you call your own. Possessions should be objects with which we have a connection. If you dote on a wire cage with a stuffed canary inside, that's fine. If your life is filled with objects that are meaningless to you, you will always be unhappy.

In some ways it is easier when you have nothing. When I finally bought my first studio apartment, I had just enough money for a frying pan, a deck chair, one set of bed linen, and a desk lamp. The last was an optimistic purchase because I didn't have a desk.

Of course, the modern medicine for unhappiness is spending. When people are left to start again — new home, or old home stripped of its past by an abrupt exit, the obvious answer is shopping. I think that is a disaster. If you can tell me a story about every single thing in your house, then you have a home. Anyone can go shopping, but meaning cannot be bought. But you can try to buy something simple and beautiful that you will always love — a cup for your morning coffee, a vase for flowers, a lamp that stands for light in all its meanings.

Private magic is about investing ordinary objects with talismanic power. Children do it all the time, and adults forget to do it at all.

I once stayed in a strange castle with the sculptor Antony Gormley.

The first thing he did was to turn the portraits of Scottish ancestors face to the wall. Then he asked us all to make some quick drawings of our own to pin gently onto the brown paper backs of the banished pictures. Next he went outside and hauled in driftwood to lighten and subvert the heavy Gothic furniture. Then he found a dozen eggcups, and turned them upside down to act as candleholders. Most people would leave the eggcup the right way up and stand the candle in it — making it look studenty and rather sad. But with a magic twist of the wrist, Gromley turned crockery into a table decoration with a purpose.

This was another form of private magic — the alchemy that shifts one thing into another. If you are unhappy, or vulnerable, or hurt, or lost, it is still possible to live in or to create a happy home. This isn't sleight of hand, it is magic at its most sympathetic.

And because it is magic, what can't be done is a version of the past. The thing has to be new, different, unafraid, even if you, the person making it, are very afraid. Fear is not a problem. Fear of fear is a huge problem. If you walk through your new front door and feel panic like the world is falling in, the first thing to do is to create a space within your new space where you will not take your misery or fear.

This can be a room, or as simple as a chair, but when you sit in that chair you can have no negative thoughts, no tears, no rage. The moment you feel anything bad, you get up from the chair. This in itself is instructive; can you feel OK for 5 minutes? An hour? All evening?

For me, the positive space is my study. I work there, I read there, but I don't stress there. If I want to cry or shout at the cat, I go somewhere else.

When I had nothing, the safe space was my little rug. I could cry myself to sleep in bed, or sit with my head in my hands at the table, but the rug, as I understand it now, was a place of informal meditation. At the time it was more like a life belt than a flying carpet, but whatever it was, it worked, because once I had named it and claimed it as a safe space, I had to believe that it was so. If you shatter the magic, it's lost — and so are you.

Gradually, if you have one safe calm space, the bigger space around you becomes safe and calm too. It is important to make some rules for yourself about your home and you inside it, and if you live by those rules, they will work for you. This takes thought, planning, self-awareness, courage, and a sense of humour. You don't need a big budget or a TV show that helps you 'create' 'your' space. Rather, you need a space inside to project onto the space outside. *Inner houses, outer houses,* as my Jewish friends tell me.

Happy/normal. Normal/happy. Home is where the questions are answered well. The home you make should have a rightness to it that makes you feel good about yourself.

I know from my own experience that the little world we build just beyond our bodies, the intimate place that we call home, is the one place in the wide world where we should be able to be ourselves — contradictory, wayward, odd, timid, bold, afraid sometimes, unhappy sometimes, but look, there's the painting you found when... the curtains you made from... the table you bought that day... the book open by the bed... those flowers from the market... the jars of pasta and rice... the cushions in a heap... the wine glasses that don't match... the rug on the floor.

My little rug is still with me. It has gradually unravelled as my life has come together. The threads are loose, the loom-work visible, but the colours are still bright and strong. It was probably a hundred years old when I bought it, and thirty years have been added since. It hasn't been well-treated, but it has been well-loved.

And if I had to grab a bag and run for my life, my little rug would be the one thing I wouldn't leave behind. It is both memory and courage. Part broken, part whole, you begin again. ■

Jeanette Winterson is the author of Sexing the Cherry *and* Oranges Are Not the Only Fruit, *among other novels.*

CONISTON, CUMBRIA *Out from under.* Just above their farmhouse, Dorothy Wilkinson and husband, Glenn, join their dog, Moss, in herding their Herdwick sheep. Herdwicks are among the hardiest breeds, well equipped to survive on the high fells of the Lake District. 'We really enjoy shepherding our sheep, there's no better way of life,' says Dorothy. 'We just wish we were out here the whole time, instead of having to deal with the legislation and paperwork that are the bane of our lives.' In the 17th century, wool fabrics were responsible for more than two-thirds of England's foreign trade. Today, the world's leading wool producers are China, Australia, New Zealand, and Argentina. 📷 Justin Leighton

WEST END, EDINBURGH *Brush up.* Standing at four feet two, chimney sweep Albert Boat, 48, has been a circus clown and appeared as a Jawa in *Star Wars*. These days he works as a sweep with an Edinburgh company, Auld Reekie. Albert is joined on the rooftop by Kirk McLenaghan, 37, who owns the company, and Sid Mutch, 40. Edinburgh Castle dominates the skyline. In the 1960s there were 300–400 sweeps in the city. Now there are only a handful. 📷 **Murdo MacLeod**

[Age is a significant factor in determining whether individuals are likely to go online in the UK:
only 29 percent of those over age 65 said they use the Internet,
the figure for those aged 16–24 was 96 percent.]

GODMANCHESTER, CAMBRIDGESHIRE *Sole brothers.* When Oliver Bridge, 18, couldn't find shoes to fit his size 13 feet, he decided to open an online business, 'Bigger Feet', to sell large-sized shoes — and won the 2005 Enterprising Young Brit Award. Now studying at Oxford, he recently sold the business, which shifts about 60 pairs a month, and which he runs from his bedroom, to his 16-year-old brother, Tom. Oliver says he sold it for a snip at £1,500 because he wants to keep the business in the family.   ◎ Mischa Haller

BATTERSEA, LONDON *A new crew.* Belying media stereotypes, most of the five-strong Infa-Red Crew are university students or have full-time jobs. Sulphur, 22 (right), says, 'It's about life. Black kids are killing each other right, left, and centre — there's no good reason for this. The right music can help them understand where they're going wrong.' Who (far left) plays drums, and MC Kiss (left) writes the words. 📷 Simon Wheatley

NORTHOLT, MIDDLESEX. *Rhyme scheme.* In a friend's home studio in north London, hip hop singer, rapper and writer Andre Sinclair, 24 (also known as Tower of Knowledge), is recording his first album. He has grown up with music around him all his life — his dad is also a musician. Andre has studied music management and says he is hoping to become a musical role model and use his music to do something positive for young people. 📷 Julien Creff

PORTSMOUTH, HAMPSHIRE *Lost dimension.* Beltane Jackson, 81, is a painter and sculptor. One of his sculptures — *The Three Graces: Miss Grace, Lady Grace and Disgrace* — stands on the campus at the University of Winchester. Before his son, Nicholas, who was 48, died last year, Beltane and his wife Sylvia flew to Canada to be with him for his last months. The loss has almost crippled Beltane's ability to sculpt — and so, since then, working in his garden shed/studio, he paints instead. 📷 Vicki Couchman

HACKNEY, LONDON *Chain store.* Adam Rider, 27, started out running a bicycle workshop for homeless people, teaching them the mechanics of bicycles and their repair. He then decided to set up his own repair shop, which he now runs from the front room of his home, although he's looking for bigger premises. Keeping it in the family, Adam shares a house with his brother, who runs a music studio from an upstairs bedroom. 📷 David Modell

ISLE OF SKYE, INVERNESS-SHIRE *Shadow play.* Part-time chimney sweep Alan Squires, 58, puts on a base of paint in preparation for winter. 'This morning it was beautiful,' he says, 'but by lunchtime there was a very strong wind and rain — and that finished me for the day.' Alan moved to the island from York in 1987. He has no regrets: 'There's a community spirit you just don't get in England. I never have to advertise for work, it's word of mouth. Everybody knows everybody.' 📷 Richard Baker

SACOMBE, HERTFORDSHIRE *Recovery room.* When property developer Crispin Vaughan bought his home 14 years ago it was a museum, with the family living in a corner of the second floor. 'I knew I wanted it as soon as I walked through the door,' he recalls. Today it serves as both his home and his office. 'I grew up in a nice manor house in Gloucestershire, but when I was nine years old I stayed in the amazing house of my friend from prep school, and ever since I've wanted to live in a house like this. I've no plans to move; it's where I want to be.' 📷 Leonie Purchas

ABERGAVENNY, MONMOUTHSHIRE *Draped.* Patricia and Charles Lester run a design studio from their home, where they hand dye, embroider and pleat £3,000 dresses sold at Harrods to celebrities and royalty. Elizabeth Taylor recently wore one of their dresses for her birthday party. They also design wedding dresses, film costumes, tapestries, bedcovers, cushions, throws, screens and curtains. Each piece of cloth is hand painted in much the same way as an artist might create a rich and luminous garment. Patricia's father was a direct descendant of Hereward the Wake, upon whose exploits some of the legend of Robin Hood was based. 📷 Steve Peake

PLUMSTEAD, LONDON *Money shot.* Author, ex-gangster and celebrity Dave Courtney, 48, plays pool at his home, which he refers to as 'Camelot', as his driver, Ted, keeps watch. Once known as the Yellow Pages of the Underworld because he knew the whereabouts of criminals near and far, Courtney says he has left crime and now raises money for charity. But he still has his connections: 'This is a very hectic and busy house,' he says. 'It's important to a lot of people. And everything about it suits my character — including the weird and wonderful characters that walk through the door.' 📷 Jocelyn Bain Hogg

In England and Wales the risk of becoming a victim of crime has decreased nearly 50 percent over the past 10 years.

Princess. Courtney de Courtney, 10, is the youngest of Dave's six children. 'She absolutely loves it here,' says Dave. 'She thinks it's a circus —and she's right. She's not intimidated by anything or anyone, even if they're big, tall and scary.' As for his former life, Dave says, 'It wasn't being a villain I found addictive, it was the lifestyle around it.' 📷 Jocelyn Bain Hogg

CARNFORTH, CUMBRIA *Parked up.* Gerry McLaughlin, 48, has been a long-distance driver for two years. When he's on the road he sleeps in the cab of his lorry. 'It's solitary, but comfortable,' he says. 'It's warm and I've got a TV; I've even got Freeview.' Some truck stops are better than others, Gerry says, and he avoids the worst ones. 'I meet quite a few work colleagues at night,' he says, and often joins them for a cup of tea. Then it's back on the road in the morning for the rest of the five-day average trip. When Gerry isn't on the road, his home is in the Scottish Borders, where he lives with his wife, Linsey, 46, a nurse. ◎ Ivor Prickett

FARINGDON, OXFORDSHIRE *Boot camp.* Mike Scott, 44, is Huntsman of the Old Berkshire Hunt and is responsible for more than 50 foxhounds plus the management of the kennels and staff. 'We hunt within the law by laying trails of fox-based scent for hounds to hunt,' he says. 'We have the full co-operation of the farmers and landowners.' Though he lives and works in the same place, home is still a special place. 'When my daughter greets me at the door with a hug it completely dissolves any troubles at work and puts things in perspective,' he says. 📷 Justin Leighton

HOMEBOUND

I GOT HOME THE OTHER EVENING after two weeks away in the USA. Even as I stepped from the door of the aircraft on to the gantry I felt as if I was home: the grey frayed carpeting, the crap-flat lighting, the odour of Heathrow Airport — the busiest in Europe — was at once chilly and cloacal, suggesting the presence of many thousands of — albeit invisible — bodies.

It doesn't sound too good this, does it? Not exactly what the Germans would term *gemütlich*, and yet I found it so. It got better — or worse — as I romped along the endless travelators, through jerry-built corridors of unspeakable drabness. At Immigration the official scanned my passport and said, chronic boredom doing battle with politeness, 'Thank you, sir.' And I was in. The echoic Heathrow Express train station, the even more cavernous Paddington, with its nineteenth-century whale's belly of glass-and-iron ceiling; then I was down, striding through the foot tunnels into the Tube. Ah! The ineffably homey London Tube: I grew up in these people-funnels, their warm zephyrs freighted with a myriad cold viruses and food smells.

When I was a child I travelled eight stops on the Tube to get to school, a roundabout journey geographically, but in terms of time the quickest way there. On the weekends I would buy a ticket for 30 pence, and spend the whole day roaming through this subterranean world, only popping up to ground level from time to time. In winter, the surface world was so cloaked with fog, and smothered in darkness, that I had the distinct sensation that I was scuttling from lighted burrow to burrow, my twitching nose questing for air, my mole eyes blinking.

You may have the impression that I'm straying off the point here — that I'm not writing about 'home' as commonly understood, but my home town — an altogether different notion. However, in my case the two are indissoluble: home is, after all, a *gestalt*, compounded of the senses, their memories, and the mind's determination to assemble these into a harmonious whole. The point is, that from the age of nine or so, for me

London began to be my home, rather more than my parents' house.

I don't want to make a big deal about this, but mine was not an especially happy childhood. Certainly, I have happy enough memories of home when I was small, but the emphasis here has to be on 'enough'. It's also the case that those memories are a thick broth of the sensual: the touch of my mother's flannel dressing gown, my glint of father's change scattered on top of his bow-fronted chest of drawers, the smell of the puppies when they — and I — were small.

And, of course, I recall the layout, the look, the very embodiment of childhood home, with an increasingly veridical accuracy. I can sit here now and draw a floor plan that will show where my eldest brother's double-bass was propped, and where the reproduction Matisse of mussels on a plate hung. I could describe the precise characteristics of wallpaper and carpet and paint and rug; I could summon up the very tension of the springs of the beds I slept in. It's not far from where I sit typing now — only an hour by the Tube. In the past decade I've been back that way two or three times, to show my children as they've grown older.

It's not a remarkable house: a red-brick semi in a suburban street, but the most remarkable thing about it, to my eyes, was always that the driveway, with its irregular pattern of flagstones, and a chipped ridge of granite guttering, had over the decades remained exactly the same as when I came into consciousness there, as a toddler, dabbling in dirt and twigs, scratching myself on the privet hedge of the front garden.

Then, the last time I went back, a year ago, it had finally changed. The current incumbents, not content with repainting the shutters and replacing the garage door, had resurfaced the driveway. I stood there, looking down at its bluey-black expanse, obliterating my *heimat*, and felt a curious liberation: you can never return to the past, but it's as well to have the occasional door slammed in your face — simply in order to hammer this home.

As it happened, I was engaged in an unusual survey of my sense of home on that particular day. I had decided to walk from my current home, to where I was born, to my childhood home, to where I was at school — all within a few miles of each other in London — and then on to Oxford, where I was at university. There are few people, nowadays, in the mobile West whose lives are sufficiently geographically condensed to be able to do this — but I'm one of them. I wanted to connect all the principal sites of my life with the effort of my own muscles, to bind them to me physically. Looking back on the enterprise, it occurs to me that this was all part of the homemaking of London that had been going on since I was nine.

When I was nine, my father left the family home. He came back and went again a couple of times in the next eight years, but essentially, when I was nine my idea of home was irretrievably damaged. When I was 17, the family house was sold. I recall, quite distinctly, sitting in the front seat of the removals van we had hired to drive the residuum of my mother's chattels to her new flat (my elder brothers were long gone), and thinking at the time: good, I'm glad that's over, because I was, quite predictably, disgusted as much with suburbia as with what I saw as the charade of my parents' marriage.

I went away to university — I returned home. I went and lived with my father, who had made a new home for himself in Australia — but I returned to London once more. The years passed, I married, and moved out of London for a couple of years, only to come home when the marriage collapsed. And here, with the exception of some brief sojourns, I have remained ever since. In 1997 I remarried, and the past decade has seen that most strange of things: the gradual accretion of memories, and sensations, and memories of those sensations, that perfuse mere bricks and mortar and possessions, to end up, quite inevitably, creating a genuine sense of home.

Children help. To be with psyches, agglomerations of billions of neurons, which have coalesced in a particular place, is to feel that much more rooted. Two children have come as newborns to this house, and their two older half-siblings also have thought of it as a kind of home. There have been births — and anniversaries of them; parties — and the whole quotidian go-round, the wheels of domesticity leaving their hopefully happy ruts in the road.

So, here I come, listening to the Cockney accents, leafing through the free sheet — then out of the Tube station, observing the guys messing about outside the station, and then those standing, smoking, outside the local pub. My weary feet are carrying me past the curiously beautiful Modernist bus garage, then the Duke of Cambridge pub — run by Portuguese immigrants — then into my road.

The human story is one of a supercharged odyssey, as we sprinted out of Africa, populating the globe within a few millennia. Then we sat put and diverged over a few more. Racial distinctions are, as the geneticist Stanley Wells told me, comparatively recent developments in the human genome. And now, it seems, we are heading back to where we came from: jumbling-up into the undifferentiated group we once were. It's a curious irony that our very ubiquity will produce the same effect as our prior isolation.

And yet... and yet... as middle age got its grip on me, and I became prey to genealogical speculations, I discovered a curious fact about my family. It transpired that the earliest known Self to have lived in London — one Adolphus Self, a coach painter — was entered in the 1841 census as having been resident at Kennington Cross, a mere half mile from here.

So, it seems that while I may myself be one of the Modernists, with my half-Jewish, half-English blood, and while I may trot the globe, I still return to a strange kind of urban homeland: a quarter of a mighty world city in which six generations of the male line of my family have now resided.

I don't begrudge anyone coming into this Self homeland — on the contrary, the burgeoning of London's immigrant population during my adult life has been a source of delight to me. I remember this city as far duller and blander when it was more homogeneous. But the biggest source of pleasure for me is to see how all of them have been impregnated with *genus loci*: black, brown, white — they look like Londoners, they all sound like Londoners — they're perfectly at home here. And so am I.

Will Self is a novelist (The Book of Dave), *short story writer and newspaper columnist* (Junk Mail).

TYBURN CONVENT, MARBLE ARCH, LONDON *Food for the soul.* Tyburn Convent, in the noisy heart of London, was established in 1903 on the site of King's Gallows, where more than 50,000 criminals — and 105 Catholic martyrs — were executed. While the nuns pray in silent shifts, day and night, for those lost souls, the only sounds emanating from the convent are hymns sung during seven daily masses. 📷 Stuart Freedman

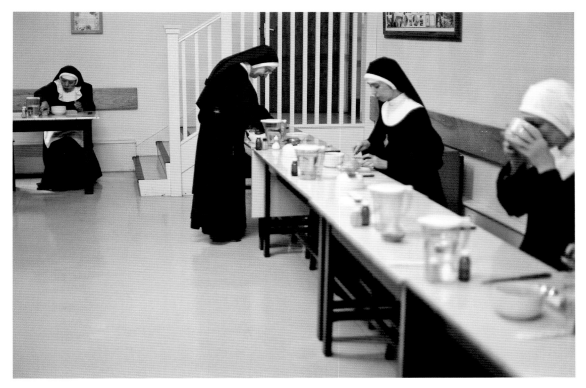

Home is a habit. Once a nun has completed her training, her devotion is a lifelong commitment and meals are largely taken in silence. Though separate from the world, the convent is still part of it: it accepts thousands of prayer petitions over the Internet. Each is printed out, is placed on the founder's tomb, and is the subject of a public prayer by the nuns. 📷 Stuart Freedman

Sporting chance. In the daily hour of recreation, Scrabble and jigsaws are both popular. Here, Sister Catherine, 22, Sister Marie-Chanelle, 25, and Sister Ruth, 27, play badminton. Conversation is allowed, but no gossip, and close friendships are strongly discouraged. 📷 Stuart Freedman

CAMBERLEY, SURREY *Details and detachment.* The Royal Military Academy Sandhurst is the only establishment for initial officer training in the British Army. All British Army officers — and many from other nations — train at Sandhurst. The academy's alumni include Princes William and Harry, the King of Tonga, the Sultan of Brunei, Ian Fleming (who failed the course) and Winston Churchill. The Colonel-in-Chief is the Queen. Here two junior-term officer cadets are in their third week of training. They will spend another 41 weeks in their new home before they become commissioned officers. 📷 Andy Hall

CAMBERLEY, SURREY *Equal opportunity.* Women comprise 10% of all students who have trained at Sandhurst since 1984. This senior-term officer cadet is just 11 weeks from becoming a commissioned officer and upon graduation she will go to specialist training. Women train alongside male cadets and are fully integrated into the academic work. 📷 Andy Hall

HM NAVAL BASE CLYDE, FASLANE *Encapsulated.* Vinnie Browse, 37, has been a submariner for seven years and his Junior Rating bunk often becomes his home away from home for three months at a time. HM Naval Base Clyde, at Faslane, is home to the UK's strategic nuclear deterrent and the headquarters of the Royal Navy in Scotland. His vessel, *HMS Vigilant*, is a Vanguard class nuclear submarine capable of circumnavigating the entire globe without surfacing and is home and workplace to 146 crew. 📷 Richard Baker

DUNVEGAN CASTLE, ISLE OF SKYE *Endurance.* Dunvegan Castle has been the stronghold of the Chiefs of the Clan MacLeod for nearly 800 years. Built on a rock once surrounded entirely by the sea, it is the only Hebridean stronghold to have retained both its family and its roof throughout the centuries. The castle is home to one of the most famous Scottish relics; the Fairy Flag. ◉ Richard Baker

Laird of the castle. Hugh MacLeod, 34, the thirtieth Chief of the Clan MacLeod, enjoys his morning tea high atop his family's centuries-old castle. In spite of intermittent periods of warring with neighbouring clans and enormous social, political and economic change, the family has been forced to leave the castle only once: during the potato famine of 1847–51.　📷 Richard Baker

Tour director. Hugh talks to Maureen M. Byers, the castle's curator. Open to visitors, the castle's stately rooms are full of artefacts and paintings that track the family's history back to medieval times. Architecturally, the castle is a unique historical record, having been altered through at least ten building periods.　📷 Richard Baker

LIVERPOOL, MERSEYSIDE *Peek-a-boo.* Stephen Seddon, 41, pops out for a fag in the back garden of his house. Stephen owns a company that fits windows and extensions — in his spare time he grows vegetables. An avid Liverpool supporter, he lives across the street from the house in which he grew up, and where his parents still live. He and his teaching assistant wife, Lorna, 35, have two sons — Ben, 3, watching television, and Johnnie, 2, watching the photographer at work. 📷 Andrew Buurman

TRINITY COLLEGE, OXFORD *Diplomatic encounter.* Former British Ambassador to Rome, Sir Ivor Roberts, 61, is President of Trinity College. He resides there with his wife Elizabeth and their spaniel, Dido. 'Living on such an historic campus is an absolute delight,' he says. 'There's physical beauty on every side and the buzz of student activity to keep us young in spirit (and awake at unusual hours in the night!)'. 📷 Mike Abrahams

DULWICH, LONDON *Rewarding work.* Jaz Bushell, 43, and her husband, David, 43, run Drape Star out of their home, and their specialty is creating atmospheric sets for corporate events. Here Jaz is making drapes for the *Q Magazine* awards. 'They are quite huge — each one about 30 ft by 10 ft,' says Jaz. 'It can take me about 30–40 minutes to make one, but I just listen to the radio and switch my mind off.' The wall behind Jaz displays lights she made out of larder doors found in a salvage yard. The pink glow comes from sheets of lighting gel placed over fluorescent tubes. 🄯 Chris Steele-Perkins

Office romance. Jaz and David met at art college when they were 17 and set up in business together in 1988 doing ultraviolet backdrops for raves. These days they often work at home on their set designs. And they dance. 'We went to Brazil a few years ago and saw some people dancing on the beach and decided we must learn,' says Jaz. 'We settled on the tango.' Here, they practise in the kitchen, while their daughter Ezme, 16, does her homework.   📷 Chris Steele-Perkins

HEBDEN BRIDGE, WEST YORKSHIRE *The tenant of Kersal House.* Walkers and visitors are fond of Maggie Stewart's guest house in Haworth, the centre of the Pennines. The Brontë sisters wrote most of their novels at the nearby Haworth Parsonage. Maggie's husband, Ron, spends much of his time in the Middle East working for a peace and reconciliation charity. Their four children, now grown up, live in different places around the world. 📷 John Angerson

" I want a house that has got over all its troubles. I don't want to spend the rest of my life bringing up a young and inexperienced house. "

– Jerome K. Jerome

BLACKSHAW HEAD, YORKSHIRE *Rooted.* Although they have lived on their farm for 30 years, Bea, 58, and her husband Max Tasker, 60, are still known locally as 'Offcumdens'— people from somewhere else. When they first arrived in this remote farm area they were overjoyed to be able to purchase a home with 6.4 acres for less than the price of a house in Bedford. And although the weather can often be bleak, they have learned to appreciate what they've got. The Taskers' children, grown up now, live in cottages belonging to the farm and Dan, their eldest son, runs the local pub. 📷 John Angerson

Dimples. Peter Hall is the owner of the Breaky Bottom vineyard, renowned for its sparkling wines. He first planted vines here in 1974 on four acres. Today he manages six acres, from which he produces his annual harvest. A sizable portion of one year's production matures in the racks behind him.　◎ Roger Bamber

Tendrils. With a climate similar to France's Champagne region, southern England is a good place to grow grapes for sparkling wines, one of the Breaky Bottom vineyard's specialities. Winemaking declined in England in the 'Little Ice Age' that began in the seventeenth century. Global warming is being credited with bringing it back.　◎ Roger Bamber

RODMELL, EAST SUSSEX *Harvest time.* Wine has been produced in the British Isles since the days of the Romans. Today, there are about 360 vineyards in the UK, the largest having 265 acres, producing a wide range of wines. The Breaky Bottom vineyard, owned by Peter Hall, is a family-run affair with friends and relatives often helping bring in the crop. During the harvest, Peter's wife, Chris, cooks up a hearty lunch for all. Despite its popularity, domestic winemakers only produce about 1% of the wine consumed each year in the UK. 📷 Roger Bamber

NEWTONMORE, INVERNESS-SHIRE *Stag night.* Douglas Langlands, head deer stalker of the Ardverikie Estates, and his pony, Henry, are met by Douglas's partner, Lorna Donald, at the door of their cottage above Kinlochlaggan. This 45,000-acre site is one of Scotland's oldest and most famous deer forests. Ponies are essential for transporting carcasses such as the stag shown here, which had been shot a few hours earlier. Douglas has lived on the estate for 34 years, Lorna for 24. 📷 Murdo MacLeod

SGEIR NAM BIAST, ISLE OF SKYE *Beacon.* A lone light glows on one of the farthest reaches of the British Isles, seemingly calling its people home from wherever they are in the world. Often called a loch, Sgeir nam Biast is, in fact, a bay that overlooks the headland called Waternish on the far north-west tip of Skye. 📷 Richard Baker

LONDON *Moonlight.* With a population exceeding 7.5 million, London is comprised of a broad range of peoples, cultures and religions. As one of the world's primary financial and cultural centres, London's impact on politics, education, entertainment, media, fashion and the arts contributes to its status as a major global city. London was the first city in the world to surpass 5 million in population, and on its crowded streets one can hear more than 300 languages spoken. 📷 Rick Smolan

ESSAYISTS

SIR PAUL McCARTNEY, MBE, born in Liverpool, is listed in the *Guinness Book of World Records* as the most successful musician and composer in popular music history. He is also a well-known advocate for animal rights, vegetarianism and retirement of Third World debt.

ALEXANDER McCALL SMITH, CBE, is a Rhodesian-born writer who resides in Scotland. An emeritus professor of medical law at the University of Edinburgh, he is the author of *The No. 1 Ladies' Detective Agency* series, *The Sunday Philosophy Club* series, and a number of children's books and academic works on medical law and bioethics.

SIMON WINCHESTER, OBE, is an author, travel writer and journalist who currently lives in the United States. A onetime foreign correspondent for *The Guardian*, he is the author of such works of history as *The Surgeon of Crowthorne* and *The Map That Changed the World*, as well as a number of travel books, including *Outposts: Journeys to the Surviving Relics of the British Empire*.

ALAIN DE BOTTON, who was raised in London, is an essayist, novelist and television producer, best known for his writing on philosophical subjects. Many of his books, including *The Consolations of Philosophy* and *The Architecture of Happiness*, have been turned into television documentaries.

BLAKE MORRISON, born in North Yorkshire, is professor of creative and life writing at the University of London, a fellow of the Royal Academy of Literature and a novelist. He is the author of the memoir *And When Did You Last See Your Father?*

JACKIE KAY, MBE, born in Edinburgh, is a poet, screenwriter and novelist. Her works, which often deal with cultural identity, include the poetry collections *The Adoption Papers* and *Other Lovers*. She is also the author of the novel *Trumpet*.

JEANETTE WINTERSON, OBE, is a novelist, journalist and delicatessen owner. Born in Manchester and raised in Lancashire, she currently lives in London. Her best-known novels, including *Sexing the Cherry* and *Oranges Are Not the Only Fruit*, explore the nature of gender identity.

WILL SELF, raised in London, is a novelist and journalist. He is known for his fantastical novels and short stories, including *The Book of Dave*; his reviews and columns (collected in such works as *Junk Mail*); and his television appearances on such programmes as *Grumpy Old Men*.

PHOTOGRAPHERS

To produce a project with the scope and dimension of *UK At Home*, we dispatched 50 of the UK's leading photojournalists around the nation for a week. In addition, tens of thousands of talented amateurs also took time from their busy lives to shoot and submit their photos. We'd like to thank the following professionals and all the amateurs who contributed so much talent to make this project possible.

Mike Abrahams	David Gillanders	David Levene	Ivor Prickett
Guilhem Alandry	Mike Goldwater	Alan Lewis	Leonie Purchas
John Angerson	Charlie Gray	Barry Lewis	Louis Quail
Richard Baker	Brian Griffin	Murdo Macleod	Duncan Raban
Roger Bamber	Andy Hall	Cecilia Magill	John Reardon
Thomas Brandi	Mischa Haller	Peter Marlow	Simon Roberts
Jo Broughton	Pål Hansen	Mary McCartney	Franklyn Rodgers
Andrew Buurman	Jocelyn Bain Hogg	Gideon Mendel	Rick Smolan
Edmund Clark	Roger Hutchings	Dod Miller	Tina Stallard
Vicki Couchman	Caroline Irby	Dario Mitidieri	Chris Steele-Perkins
Peter Dench	Justin Kernoghan	David Modell	Zak Waters
John Downing	Kalpesh Lathigra	David Partner	Simon Wheatley
Stuart Freedman	Justin Leighton	Steve Peake	

" Do you live in a house or a home? Are you in it for the money or the love?
Do you think you'll be happy when you move? Or are you happy now?
Does it give you financial security or emotional warmth?
Does it make you feel like you're getting somewhere?
Or does it make you feel like you're there now?
If it could talk, could it tell anyone what your favourite colour is?

When your little boy draws a plane on the wall, do you reach for the roller or grab another crayon and draw a rocket?

Is it perfect? Or is it real, and still perfect?
Do you keep it as empty as possible to create space, or do you fill it with all the people
and things you enjoy the most? Do you look in estate agents' windows?
Or do you look in your own window and think 'how lovely'?
Are you constantly monitoring its price or are you measuring its occupants' heights
on the back of the bathroom door? What's the most important thing you put into it,
two fifths of your salary, or your life and soul? What's the most important thing you'll get out?
A profit? Or a treasure trove of memories that'll never ever go down in value but always up.
It's not too late. A house can always become a home. Love, not money.
That's what gives a home a soul. And a home's soul is not for sale. "

MY HOME IS THE MOST IMPORTANT PLACE IN THE WORLD ...

My PR Manager was asking me the other day if I could write a few lines for this book about home and life at home and what this means for me. I was thinking about my home and the places I have lived.

I calculated and worked out that I have lived in 17 different places so far in my life.

In comparison I reflected on my parents who have only lived in three different places ... and my grandparents who lived in the same place all their lives! The kids of my generation will most likely live in many different places in their life. They will move for a whole host of reasons... for college and education, for jobs and their career, for the adventure, for love... or even for fun.

Thinking of the 17 different places I have lived... I have lived in a college room, in numerous rented places, both flats and houses, in my own home, in hotels and temporarily with friends and family. I have built my own house. I have bought and sold... and bought and sold again. I have lost money but I have also been lucky to make a little money too.

Some of the places I have lived are full of happy memories of great times spent there. These are the places I still call home! Because for me a 'house' becomes a 'home' when it is not just an address or a postcode. The feelings of security, peace, love, friendship, warmth, laughter, togetherness and the opportunity to just be yourself are what for me makes a HOME and how your home becomes an identity more than an investment or just bricks and mortar.

Home IS the most important place in the world... and not even because of its furniture – but because it is such an important part of our lives!

– Peter Högsted

GOOGLE

Google's mission is to organise the world's information and make it universally accessible and useful. We were drawn to the *UK at Home* project because of its focus on capturing the range of experiences and emotions associated with home and family life. We are pleased that our products were used to share the photographs from this project with a broad audience. The *UK at Home* photographers and writers have created a story that celebrates the human experience, and we are glad to have played a part in bringing this to you.

HP SNAPFISH

Snapfish has more than 45 million members worldwide and two billion unique photos stored online. Share, store and edit your photos free in a secure, password-protected account. Get professionally developed prints for just 10p each delivered straight to your door or collect them free from your local Jessops store! Plus, Snapfish offers a wide range of customisable photo products, from photo books and greeting cards to mouse pads, calendars and collage posters. Create your free account today!

BABYCENTRE

BabyCentre knows that nothing makes a house a home more than children. The *UK at Home* project is an ideal outlet to depict both the harmonies and challenges of home life with children, and thousands of our users have submitted their photos for consideration in this project. BabyCentre, the leading pregnancy and parenting website in the UK, is dedicated to being a trusted resource of information and tools for new and expectant parents.

CAMERA BITS & PHOTO MECHANIC

Founded in 1996 by Dennis Walker, Camera Bits is the developer of Photo Mechanic, the standard workflow software for digital photojournalists around the world. www.camerabits.com

DRIVESAVERS DATA RECOVERY

With the highest success rate in the data recovery industry, DriveSavers Data Recovery proves to its business, government, academic and individual customers all over the world that data loss is only temporary. www.drivesavers.com

FACEBOOK

Facebook is a social utility that connects people with friends and others who work, study and live around them. People use Facebook to keep up with friends, upload an unlimited number of photos, share links and videos and learn more about the people they meet. www.facebook.com

FILEMAKER

Millions of customers, from individuals to large organisations, rely on FileMaker's award-winning database software, which includes the legendary FileMaker Pro product line for Windows, Mac and the web, to manage, analyse and share information. FileMaker, Inc. is a subsidiary of Apple Inc. www.filemaker.com

HEWLETT-PACKARD

HP focuses on simplifying technology experiences for all its customers, from individual consumers to the largest businesses, with a portfolio that spans printing, personal computing, software, services and IT infrastructure. www.hp.com

KINETIC INDUSTRIES (PANALUX)

Created by Panalux, a world leading supplier of film & television production equipment, Kinetic provides a flexible, competitive service combining an extensive range of cameras, lights and expendables with the support of experienced, friendly staff. Substantial investment in the finest equipment ensures Kinetic has the resources to meet the demands of any photographic assignment. Kinetic is the equipment rental facility for the professional photographic industry. www.go-kinetic.com

LACIE

LaCie's external storage solutions and color monitors feature original designs and leading-edge technology to help people easily manage their digital lives. www.lacie.com

O'REILLY'S DIGITAL MEDIA

O'Reilly's Digital Media connects people to the experts through books and online resources from highly respected working professionals who are masters of tools and technologies focused on the rapidly changing world of creative media. http://digitalmedia.oreilly.com

PANTONE

Pantone, Inc. is the world-renowned provider of colour systems and leading technology for the selection and accurate communication of colour across a variety of industries. www.pantone.com

POWER ON SOFTWARE

Now Software is the developer of the Eddy Award-winning Now Up-to-Date and Contact, the number-one calendar and contact management software for business and power users. www.nowsoftware.com

TRAVELMUSE

TravelMuse provides content, community and planning tools to empower consumers to make better online travel decisions. www.travelmuse.com

STAFF AND ACKNOWLEDGEMENTS

RICK SMOLAN
Project Director

JENNIFER ERWITT
Project Director

KATYA ABLE
Chief Operating Officer

PHOTOGRAPHY ASSIGNMENTS

MICHAEL S. MALONE
Editor in Chief

JOHN EASTERBY
Photography Director

SHERIDAN McCOID
Lead Researcher

CAROLINE CORTIZO
Photographer Liaison

SHA BAINBRIDGE
Photography Assistant

ASSIGNMENT RESEARCHERS

Robert A. Grove
Daniela Hart
Simon James
Alex Ortiz
Charlotte Rowles
Jackie Stuart
Candice Temple
Regina Wolek

DESIGN & PRODUCTION

BRAD ZUCROFF
Creative Director

DIANE DEMPSEY MURRAY
Art Director

PETER TRUSKIER
Automation & Color Management

HEIDI MADISON
Project Manager

CAROLINE CORTIZO
Image Production Artist

ANN JOYCE
Production Designer

MICHAEL RYLANDER
Creative Consultant

EDITORIAL

MICHAEL S. MALONE
Caption Writer

SHERIDAN McCOID
Lead Researcher

CHARLOTTE ROWLES
Researcher

CANDICE TEMPLE
Researcher

JANE UTTING
Researcher

NARELLE DOE
Research Assistant

CAMPBELL STEVENSON
Copy Editor

PICTURE EDITORS

John Easterby
Jon Jones
  The Times
Cheryl Newman
  The Telegraph
Greg Whitmore
  The Observer
Eric Meskauskas
  Formerly *New York Daily News*
Karen Mullarkey
  Formerly *Newsweek*

TECHNOLOGY

CHUCK GATHARD
Technology Director

TOPHER WHITE
Systems Architect

WEBSITE

MICHAEL RYLANDER
Creative Director

HEATH CARLISLE
Programmer

MATTHEW REED BRUEMMER
Content Coordinator

PUBLICITY & OUTREACH

DAPHNE KIS
Communications Director

KIM SHANNON
Communications Manager

AVENUE MARKETING & COMMUNICATIONS
Mike Hettwer
Daniel Bodde

OFFICE ADMINISTRATION

ALLY MERKLEY
Office Manager

PARISA MORID
Office Manager

NANCY MERKLEY
Office Coordinator

LEGAL COUNSEL

NATE GARHART
Coblentz, Patch, Duffy & Bass, LLP

JONATHAN HART
Dow, Lohnes & Albertson, PLLC

DAVID WITTENSTEIN
Dow, Lohnes & Albertson, PLLC

SENIOR BUSINESS ADVISOR

BARRY REDER

SENIOR ADVISORS

Marvin and Gloria Smolan
Phillip Moffitt
James Able
Colin Jacobson
Cotton Coulson

LITERARY AGENT

CAROL MANN
The Carol Mann Agency

ACCOUNTING & FINANCE

EUGENE BLUMBERG
Blumberg & Associates

ARTHUR LANGHAUS
KLS Associates

JOE CALLAWAY
KLS Associates

ROBERT POWERS
Calegari & Morris Certified Public Accountants

HEIDI LINK
Calegari & Morris Certified Public Accountants

LINDA SEABRIGHT
Bookkeeper

DOCUMENTARY

David Prever
Jonathan Potts
Andy Knox
Faye
Duncan Curtis
Jason Gairn
Julian Lewis

DUNCAN BAIRD PUBLISHERS

Duncan Baird
Lucie Baird
Duncan Carson
Adela Cory
Vicky Hartley
Alex Mitchell
Anna Randall
Bob Saxton
Roger Walton

PRE-PRESS & PRINTING

GARY HAWKEY
iocolor

PETER TRUSKIER
Artist

ROBB CARR
Artist

MICHAEL RACZ
Artist

MIKE STRICKLER
MSP Graphics Inc.

ANDREW CLARKE
Asia Pacific Offset

SPONSOR

IKEA
Our Customers
Our Co-workers

ADDITIONAL SUPPORT

GOOGLE
Sergey Brin
Marissa Mayer
Lorranie Twohill
Dan Cobley
Obi Felten
Anita Rajeswaren
Michaela Prescott
Chewy Trewhella

SNAPFISH
Ben Nelson
Nicola Anderson
Geoff Ayres
Sinyen Be
Heather Calvosa
Julian Carlisle
Cass Carrigan
Deanna Dawson
Matt Domenici
Kevin Frisch
Ramana Murthy Garugu
Vijay Gatadi
Tina Hui
Hema Kannan
Sumant Manda
Murali Nallana
Ben Nelson
Rand Newman
Adina Nystrom
Dennis Prince
Shankar Ramamoorthy
David Saxton
Jay Shek
Lisa Sterling
Rolf Wilkinson

BABYCENTRE
Colleen Hancock
Nissa Anklesaria
Cynthia Maller

CAMERA BITS & PHOTO MECHANIC
Dennis Walker

DRIVESAVERS DATA RECOVERY
Scott Gaidano
Chris Lyons
John Christopher

FACEBOOK
Katie Geminder

FILEMAKER
Kevin Mallon

LACIE
Martha Humphrey
Barry Katcher

POWER ON SOFTWARE
Donn Hobson
Sean Boiarski

TRAVELMUSE
Kevin Fliess
Eric Wood
Cyril Bouteille
Donna Airoldi
Michael Kwatinetz

KINETIC FACILITIES (PANALUX)
Andy Bone
Amanda Sissons

SPECIAL THANKS

Monica Almeida
Jane Anderson
Chris Anderson
Bob Angus
Dave Armon
The Bakst Family
Simon Barnett
Sunny Bates
Belgrave House Security
Keith Bellows
Lisa Bernstein
Boat Gypsies
David Bohrman
Jessica Brackman
Russell Brown
Tess Canlas
Anne Carey
Bruce Chizen
David E. Cohen
Joyce Deep
Gene and Gayle Driskell
Dan Dubno
The Durham Family
Amy Erwitt
David Erwitt
Elliott Erwitt
Ellen Erwitt
Erik Erwitt
Misha Erwitt
Sasha Erwitt
Harlan Felt
Kevin Foong
Pia Frankenberg
Peter Friess
Mary Anne Golon
Google Canteen Staff
Mick Greenwood
Roz Hamar
Greg Harper
Michael Hawley
Kathleen Hazelton-Leech
Jerry Held
Chandi Hemapala
James Higa
Sam and Kate Holmes
Mark Hurst
Paul and Lindsey Iacovino
George Jardine
James and Zem Joaquin
Steve Jobs
Jon Kamen
Paul Kent
Matt Kursh
The Lester Family
Andrea Lovitt
Davis Masten
Lucienne Matthews
Richard Matthews
Michele McNally
Charles Melcher
Doug and Tereza Menuez
Caroline Metcalf
Nora and Hugh Moss
Matthew H. Murray
Bethany Obrecht
Dean and Anne Ornish
Rick Pappas
Alan Parker
Paula Parrish
Gabe Perle
Gabriella Piccioni
Gina Privitere
Natasha and Jeff Pruss
Pamela Reed
Steven Riggio
Peter Rockland
Diane Rylander
Sheri Sarver
Terry Schaefer
Duane Schultz
Richard Sergay
Kim Small
Rodney Smith
Leslie Smolan

Sandy Smolan
Arabella Stein
Brian Storm
Derrick Story
Aidan Sullivan
Kara Swisher
Phil Terry
Anne Wojcicki
Claudia Zamorano

FACT SOURCES

BBC News
Channel Four Television Corporation
Daily Express
Henley Centre HeadlightVision
Jane
The Office for National Statistics
United Kingdom Tourism Survey
Tim Wardle, *In Search of Mr Average*
Steve Wright's Further Factoids
Whitaker's Almanack
www.ambernaturally.com
www.coolquiz.com
www.edenproject.com
www.PersonnelToday.com
www.polity.uk.co
www.statistics.gov.uk
www.trakkies.co.uk

JUNIOR ADVISORS

Phoebe Smolan
Jesse Smolan
Alexandra Able
Zachary Able
Sophia Able
Reed Smolan
Lily Smolan
Savannah Smith
Sydney Pruss
Evan Pruss
Mason Rylander
Annabelle Rylander
CJ Erwitt
Sam Worrin
Max Worrin
Violet O'Hara
Jack Robert Boyt
Zoe Dubno
Teddy Dubno

MORALE OFFICER

Ally the Dog